TRUCKIN' THE SKIES

Alaskan Aviation Stories

By Gary Tupper

TRUCKIN' THE SKIES

Alaskan Aviation Stories

By Gary Tupper

©2018 Gary Tupper

Edited by Connie Tupper

Cover design by Gary Tupper

Production design by Robert Jacobson

Published by:
Alaska Dreams Publishing
www.alaskadp.com

1ST Print Edition June 2018

PRINT ISBN numbers:
ISBN-13: 978-0-9903454-6-6
ISBN 10: 0-9903454-6-7

E-Book versions available.
Please visit http://www.alaskadp.com for links.

CONTENTS

Electra Tanker

FOREWORD

I had the distinct pleasure of flying with Gary from the time he started as a loadmaster. We were both new to the Lockheed Electra, he as a load master and me as a First officer. From there our careers seemed to keep matching up. In 1977 times in Alaska were fast and crazy in the business of moving freight all over the state but especially the North Slope. Great Northern Airlines was always in the air with one to four aircraft around the clock.

Gary was a quick study and figured out right away that if the planes weren't in the air no one made any money. There are some people who have a work ethic that brings the best out of them. Tup is one of those guys. I never had a load shift that he put on any airplane we flew.

There are lots of different types of loadmasters such as guys who hook igloo's and pre-loaded pallets on 747s and military aircraft and maybe load a drive on now and then. While these guys have great skills and are good at what they do, they are at a loss when loading parts and pieces of a drill rig sitting on a frozen lake in the windy dark arctic night. During the pipeline and Husky oil petroleum reserve, we would move entire drill rigs, all the camps, offices, trucks, loaders, fuel, and food so they could be set up and drill a well, cap it off and take it all down and fly it to the next drill sight. This was usually done in a 3 to 4-week period start to finish. It compares to moving a small city to a frozen lake, building it and then moving it to another site many miles away.

We flew in horrendous weather with little to no navigation aids in those days. Everyone depended on each other to stay alive. Often there was no air traffic control, so we provided our own separation. It was a time of get it done, be as safe as possible, but get it done. Our mantra was "load 'em heavy, fuel 'em light, send them out in the dark arctic night".

Gary was always innovative and quick to get the loads on and off. If we weren't in the air, we didn't make any money for the company or ourselves. When I had Tup for my load master I often got an extra trip in per shift and that equaled a bigger pay check.

When Gary told me he was writing a book I did not know what to think about it. Often when pilots write books they water down what really happened. (Something about statues of limitations) Gary, not being a pilot and being about as straight forward of a guy as I've ever meet, is not worried about those pesky types of things. Besides he, like me, is retired. He calls it the way he sees it and, believe me, it's not PC! As I read the manuscript I was really taken back to those days. It is bitter sweet as it was a great time and we learned how to survive but I don't want to go back there again.

This book is a must read if you are interested in real Alaskan aviation history. It's written as if you were standing around the hanger with a bunch of old time pilots and loadmasters remembering the glory days. My hats off to you Gary, another job well done!

My apologies for taking so long, it's a great book. Finally, someone who got it right! Thanks for letting me be part of it.

Mike "RED DOG" Redmon
Chief Pilot – Retired
Lynden Air Cargo

INTRODUCTION

The flying weather was bad, the crew made it worse. Some people shouldn't drive; some people shouldn't be pilots.

Cobblestone was an exploratory drill site in the northern foothills of the Brooks Range, a beautiful place in the light of day, a dangerous proposition in the dark of night. We flew to the north of the high cloud cover over the mountains and airstrip and descended over the flatness of the North Slope. Coming around to the south we flew up the valley and its **sharp** dog leg to the left which would bring us to the runway.

I didn't have my headset on as it was a crew with little worthwhile chit-chat. The landing gear was down and flaps full when all of a sudden, we went to flaps 50%, gear up, and max power trying to spiral up between mountains in the pitch-black darkness. What the...?

With 48,000 pounds of cargo onboard you do not gain altitude very fast.

We didn't find mountains, 'cause I'm here today to write this. As we were approaching the runway the pilot thought he saw an airplane taking off straight towards us, even though the tower had cleared us to land. There was no airplane, just deadly confusion.

It's no wonder they made me put "gray" under hair color on my driver's license at the tender age of 35.

It was just another day on the job for a man called "loadmaster", a job some people quit after a couple of trips to the Alaskan bush. They felt there were better and safer options available for employment, showing more sense than I ever had. But I've always believed if you've never done anything, when the story telling starts, all you'll be doing is listening.

Truckin' The Skies is a story of moving cargo by air. An occupation that has employed many people in one way or another since aviation started.

The C-130 Hercules was intended from the start to move cargo not people, but the military uses it for both.

Southern Air Transport flew the only commercial and FAA approved combination C-130. It had a passenger pod installed in the front of the cargo compartment with the back half for cargo. This "combi" was used in Alaska and during the Bosnian war in the mid '90s. The Herc is the longest run production aircraft of any kind. First flown in 1954 and still being made today, it is literally a truck in the sky.

With 3,800 hours on a Lockheed Electra and around 25,000 hours flying time on the Herc I have accumulated some experiences and stories that will hopefully entertain and inform you about what the job, myself and others have done for years is like.

All branches of the military have always had a loadmaster as an essential part of the flight crew; commercial use of the Herc is no exception. Because of the enormous diversity of what a Herc can haul, it takes one man trained to handle it. On a lot of airplanes, the flight crew load, secure, and fly the plane. Flying the Herc in the conditions and landing on remote airstrips is enough to learn. Loading and off-loading a Herc is something you never stop learning. The discovery of oil on Alaska's North Slope was one of the main reasons the C-130 Herc came into commercial use. The C-46, DC-3, Sky Vans and other cargo planes of the time could not possibly haul the size, type and quantity of equipment and supplies needed for the construction and oil production in such a remote location.

Before the construction of the "Haul Road," today known as the Dalton Highway, flying and the occasional ocean barge in the summertime were the only means of transporting supplies to the oilfields. There have been songs sung, stories told, and books written about the treacherous Haul Road, but as far as I know, nobody has written about the flying end of moving massive amounts of supplies to the North Slope.

When I started working on the Herc for Alaska Int'l Air in 1980 oil was already flowing down the pipeline. I missed out on being one of the pioneers of "Hercing" supplies to the North Slope, but it was from these remarkable loadmasters that I learned my trade. Lessons learned the hard way were passed on to me and others by spending time flying with those who had "been there, done that." On the job training was the only real way to learn the trade. Picking up bits and pieces from different loadmasters that were filed away between the ears was the best way to learn the job. Luckily in my case, there was plenty of empty space available.

Looking for new oilfields was hot and heavy at this time so moving entire drill rigs and complete camp set-ups kept us very busy. After that, with Alaska's oil revenue wealth, it was the rebuilding and new construction of all the Native villages that kept us flying around the clock. Interspaced with summer fish hauls, equipment to remote goldmines, regular freight shipments to villages, and the always "hot" shipments to Prudhoe Bay kept the Herc in need in Alaska.

As Alaska Herc work declined worldwide business was sought after. With Southern Air Transport (SAT) I was pulled out of Alaska to fly all around the globe. A ringing phone would cancel Christmas plans, a weekend BBQ, or any other normal aspect of life. My wife would certainly vouch for planning anything. Even an evening meal could be traded for a quick trip to the airport to catch up with a Herc somewhere in the world. All this was part of the job working for a charter airline.

As any traveling salesman will tell you, flying commercial airlines was the worst part of the job. Unfamiliar airports, cramped airplanes, and different hotel room every night certainly was not the glamorous part of the job, if indeed there was any glamour to it.

Remember in the movie "Top Gun" when the pilots were threatened to be demoted to "hauling rubber dog shit from Hong Kong?" While I've never hauled rubber dogs or rubber dog shit, I have hauled real sled dog teams and what they left behind was real too. When people learn of my profession, they often ask "what do you haul?" My answer was always "what haven't we hauled?" It would make a shorter list. Let's see, what haven't we hauled? We haven't hauled an atomic bomb, but we have hauled missiles to Switzerland, we haven't hauled "lions and tigers and bears," oh wait, we have hauled a bear, but that's a story for a later chapter. Let's see, dynamite, school bus, giraffes, whales, BMW's, Kenworth's, gasoline, cyanide, people, no! We've hauled all of those too. Sorry, can't think of anything we haven't hauled, memory fails me again.

The same goes with "where do you fly it?" Like Johnny Cash sings "I've been everywhere man." Though Hercs have flown everywhere, I've personally missed out on Siberia, Antarctica, and a few countries in between. It was a see the world job. It was a chance to see and experience many different cultures and places, the tourist traps, the jungles, the deserts, the cities, the devastation of hurricanes, earthquakes and floods, and the desolation of the North Slope, always the North Slope!

Many of my friends over the years have jokingly said "I'd kill to have your job." I've always thought it was the best job I've had. There were the times I was just plain tired of it though. My friends weren't there when the load didn't want to come on or off and the chill factor was a -100°. They weren't there when the heat and humidity of the jungle would take your breath away, or when the load hadn't showed up and you spent hours in a dingy cargo office drinking terrible coffee and waiting. I don't believe there's a job in existence that doesn't get to you after a while. Hell, I'll bet a guy could even get tired of fitting bras on runway models after a while. Well... maybe not.

It has been said the definition of flying is hours and hours of sheer boredom interspaced by moments of sheer terror. Very true! When the weather was clear the scenery of Alaska, Africa, the Andes Mountains of South America and Europe's cities and the Alps would easily pass the time. When the dark of night or inclement weather obscured everything, out came the books and magazines or writing a letter to the girlfriend. Never was there any discussion of how the company was screwing us over, never, I swear! In my flight bag was a set of files, sandpaper and a supply of exotic wood or ivory that I liked to carve wildlife out of to pass the time. Flight times could run anywhere from 10 minutes, giving little time to keep up on paperwork, to a 12-13 hour leg, giving us ample time to solve all the world's problems.

Ah paperwork, another curse of aviation. Many people believe it's the wings and engines that keep an airplane aloft, it's my contention that paperwork and rumors are what keeps an airplane flying. Paperwork in triplicate or worse helped keep more people confused. I hated paperwork and none of the airlines I worked for opted to have a cute little secretary fly with us. Paperwork was left up to the co-pilot and me and the co-pilots aren't cute. The paperwork had to be accurate too, when hazardous material forms asked for signatory and title, writing Joe Blow, bigshot, didn't work and might even get you in a lot of trouble. I mean, so I've heard.

Thankfully paperwork was only a small part of the job as loadmaster. Figuring out how to get an object on or off the airplane without damaging the aircraft, people around, or the object itself, with the equipment available, was the biggest part. I'll have to admit some of my best laid plans worked out better for mice than men loading airplanes. But overall, my ideas were good; otherwise I wouldn't have held the job for so many years.

A couple of other things the job entailed were making sure the load was balanced and that it was secured to not move. Nothing could ruin your day quicker than landing and finding the load in the cockpit with you. It has happened, thankfully not to me.

Over the years I've met many people in this line of work. Between flight crews, ground handlers, fuelers, mechanics, and project managers it was countless. Though there were many names, I won't be using them in this book for a few reasons. One is that in most cases I don't remember who was there in what event, two, sometimes they wouldn't want their name used for obvious reasons, and three, I'm not much of a name dropper, I didn't work in Hollywood.

Since this is an introduction, it wouldn't be complete without relating my introduction to the job.

While looking for work at Alaska Int'l Air, a friend told me that Great Northern Air might be hiring, so I stopped at their Fairbanks office and left my name and phone number. A few days later they called saying I was hired and would call when they needed me.

The phone rang around 10 pm one night with a man saying "show up at midnight with a flashlight" to start work. This should have been my first clue it was a "fly by night" outfit. I gathered my winter gear, a flashlight, and some extra survival gear. I knew we would be heading north so that seemed like a good idea. It was!

It was a cold, dark November night when I arrived at the dispatch office. Within minutes the mechanic and I were headed down to the fuel pit to meet the airplane. It seemed everything was done in a hurry, and it was from then on. Airplanes don't make money sitting on the ground.

Pretty soon the green and yellow Lockheed Electra came taxiing in from the dark to the dimly lit fuel pit. With only two of the four engines roaring loudly it made a 180° turn and parked in front of us. To me it was big, impressive, and scary, all at the same time.

The large cargo door just behind the cockpit was opening up, revealing to me for the first time the interior of the airplane I was destined to spend many hours in. An aluminum ladder was being slid down to the ground followed by a 1" hemp rope. The rope, I found out later, was for hanging on to for dear life when the ladder slipped out from under you on the ice.

The mechanic hustled me up the ladder with him right behind me. He introduced me to the loadmaster and hurried into the cockpit to see if anything needed fixing on the airplane. The loadmaster whose name was … (what did I tell you) said "here let me show you around, do you have a flashlight?" "Yah, I do." "Good."

N404 GN had seven individual white fuel tanks, 3 long narrow tanks down each side of the fuselage and one short one in the tail. As we headed down the center aisle with his flashlight bobbing here and there he said, "Here's the main valves, open them, then these tank valves, fill them first." "Which ones?" "Then open the next valves and tanks, put 700 gals in each tank, see the sight tubes?" "No." "Right here! Oh, and don't forget to open the air valve over there." "Where?" "Be sure to shut all valves before you take off." "When?" "Let's go outside and I'll show you the rest."

Down the ladder we flew, "Here's where you hook up the SPR." "What's a SPR?" "The fuel hoses and the tail stand are here in the belly compartment. You hook the tail stand under the tail." I grabbed the tail stand and followed the bouncing flashlight into the darkness.

"Here's where you hook the tail stand, oh by the way, there's where you turn the hydraulic valve on to start the pump for offloading." The pinpoint of the flashlight hit somewhere on the belly for a split second. "Then you go back up inside, open valves and turn the pump on, it's by the cockpit." "What, where, when, how?" "Shit, my rides leaving, gotta go, see ya in the morning."

As I sit here today looking back, I have to believe that was hardly a FAA approved training course.

I went back up the ladder and slowly went back through the system shining my flashlight where it did some good. The fueler was on the ground impatiently yelling "Are you ready?" "Ahhh... not yet."

I was pretty sure the flight crew would prefer the 4,200 gallons of diesel fuel in the tanks and not sloshing around the fuselage somewhere, so I waited until I had a pretty good idea of how to go about loading before I yelled "O.K. turn it on."

Well, I got the fuel on, nothing blew up and the plane didn't tip over. So far, so good, what next? "Shut the door, idiot." The new flight crew was already in the cockpit preparing for departure, so I tackled the door "Let's see, here's a switch." The switch was right next to the door and labeled just like a garage door switch. "Up-down, good!" Even I knew the difference between up and down.

I had the door down and was trying to figure out the latch when the cockpit door opened and out came the flight engineer. "Here let me show you how that works." "Really!?" "Make sure this light is out, you can check it by pushing it in, I'll show you. "You're kidding." "Come on in the cockpit, your seats up here."

I followed him in and sat down on the little piece of fabric between two pipes he referred to as my "seat". I've sat on more comfortable boards. When I started looking around, the first thing I noticed was the little sawed-off Eskimo in the left seat right in front of me. That was the third or fourth time that night serious doubts arose about my "new job".

That sawed-off Eskimo was Holger Jorgansen, known Alaska wide as "Jorgy". I didn't know it at the time, but he was a legend and I was in the most capable hands of any captain I've had the pleasure to fly under in all my years as a loadmaster. He has since earned my utmost respect and has saved the day more than once. His ability and knowledge of Alaska and flying in it is beyond compare.

He was and is my hero! No disrespect Jorgy, but the only other hero I ever had is Yosemite Sam.

The author –
Gary "Tup" Tupper

Jorgy, Doing What He Did Best

CHAPTER 1 - THE JOB

I was unemployed at the time I applied for the job at Great Northern Airlines (GNA). Little did I know then, with that application, that for the next 30 years, off and on, loadmaster would be my occupation. Whoever came up with that title? It always made me feel a little apprehensive. I was never a "master" over anyone, anything, or any endeavor in life. "Load" I understood, it's a four-letter word and I know lots of them.

The job was moving cargo from one place to another. Since the beginning of time, at least since the wheel, nothing was ever where it was needed. That's good; it's given many people a living over the years.

Airplanes, upon invention, were first used to haul freight; passengers were hard to come by those first years. I think even Wilbur and Orville, had they known for sure they would get airborne, would have at least carried a roll of toilet paper on the very first flight. It was one item added to my "survival gear".

Meanwhile "back on the Slope." Oilfield hauling was what most of us got our start on. Massive amounts of equipment and supplies were needed before oil production could ever begin. Gravel airstrips were carved out of barren tundra terrain and the airlift began.

There's a photograph in the Alaska Airlines terminal in Deadhorse of the early days offloading a Herc. Behind the airplane are some large timbers and a D-9 cat plowing up snow for a makeshift ramp. It was a learning experience at every turn to handle the outsized Herc loads. With minimal equipment and facilities, it must have been trying times.

People had to put together a system to handle the cargo efficiently. There were many trial and error methods loadmasters had to refine. Over time a roller and skid system became the mode of operation for the C-130 Herc. Self-propelled vehicles were driven in on planks for track vehicles and on rubber tires if so equipped. Many things were just plain man-handled out the door.

The skid and roller system worked for most cargo and is still the basic method used today. A skid is basically a huge metal sled. Most skids were built from 6" box steel consisting of two runners 32 feet long tapered up at both ends. Then 8' long cross members were welded to the runners at 6' intervals and partially countersunk on the runners for added strength and to minimize height loss for cargo. This was the original design until a flaw was discovered.

Well casings, drill stems, and all sizes and lengths of pipe were a major commodity being hauled to the oilfields. The pipe was placed on the skid and chained down, much like you would see on a semi-trailer on the highway. Then the skid was winched onto the airplane and chained down. All was going well on one of the first pipe load flights to the slope, that is until the landing. After touchdown the props were reversed, and the brakes applied. While the skid remained tight, the pipe broke loose and went through the nose of the airplane onto the runway. The flight crew was busy dodging their own load. This was considered an error.

After that incident all skids had a very strong headboard welded to the front of the skid. Roughly 5 feet high and covered with expanded metal, it held everything from going forward. The headboard also helped to get a good start at building straight, square loads of lumber, crates, pallets or anything else to be hauled.

Some of the time a full 32-foot skid would cause a waste of space, so half and three-quarter length skids were made. These were extremely helpful if a mixed load of, say, lumber and vehicles or steel tanks were hauled. Floor space was always at a premium and limited to space at hand. Nobody has, of yet, figured out how to stretch an airplane like some of the trailers truckers use.

The other part of the skid and roller system would of course be the rollers. It was also the harder part of the system to perfect. As loads of 50,000 pounds, and sometimes more, were constantly being winched over them, they had to be strong and long lasting to accommodate the punishment they were put through.

I wasn't around at the start and never did see some of the early attempts at building rollers. The ones that worked well had been in use, and cussed at, for a few years. They were tough and extremely heavy, 180 pounds, the reason for cussing every time they were moved, which was often. Even though they were the best that could be built, for two men in the welding shop it was almost a full-time job to keep them repaired or replaced.

The rollers consisted of two side rails 9' long made of 3" angle iron. Cross braces were 1" angled iron welded to the rails to keep things square and minimize twisting and bending. The rollers themselves were the secret to the success of the system. They started with a 1" shaft of solid steel in the middle, which went through holes in the side rails. Slightly larger diameters of sleeves were added with grease in between till they were 3" in diameter. The whole set up was 9' long, 12" wide, and 3 ¼" high.

A full set of rollers was 10 or 12 of them on an airplane. The rollers on the ramp were beefed up with double thickness side rails, making them heavier than your average sumo wrestler and just as hard to move. Though these rollers were mostly used right side up to winch skids on, an added bonus was they could be used upside down to put awkward cargo on and winch in the airplane.

If you think all this sounds easy, you better apply for a secretary position. Upside down rollers had a mind of their own and went everywhere except were you wanted them to go. Rollers right sides up were no picnic either. A slightly bent roller would point in any direction as a skid reached it. They constantly required an alignment as loads went in or out. We had what was called a roller hook made out of 3/8" steel dowel with a handle at the top and the bottom curved into a hook. These saved a lot of bending over and were useful for many chores on the airplane, such as helping the co-pilot find his seat.

In the summer fine gravel and in the winter ice on the floor would require each roller to be chained to the tie down rings to keep them in place. This was very time consuming and tedious, not to mention no fun at -60° because it often took bare hands to accomplish the task. A clean as possible floor was a must and required constant cleaning.

This system is tried and true and works efficiently. A skid was pulled off the airplane and the ground crew would unload it while we went for another load. Every few trips a stack of empty skids would be flown back to the point of origin and the process continued till the project was complete. The rollers stayed on the airplane at all times, at least they were supposed to. A few times they were inadvertently left behind. It's like, where do you put your hat when you leave your head behind?

One time I was to meet the Herc, take over the airplane and haul a generator to a goldmine in northern Canada. I flew into JFK in New York City and the station manager for South Air Transport (SAT) drove me to upstate New York to meet the Herc at an old military airstrip, the name of which I've long forgotten. The drive through quaint towns full of antique shops and the hardwood forests along the road reminded me of why I liked this job so well, the chance to see new and different places.

He dropped me off at the ground handler's facility and left on his return trip to NYC.

A couple of hours later the Herc landed, taxied in and the flight crew got off and headed for a hotel. I crawled on board to begin loading and be all ready when the flight crew showed up. To my dismay I looked around and there were no rollers or any pulley blocks to increase the winch pulling power. Since none of us there were strong enough to carry a 30,000-pound generator on board we were dead in the water.

I went back to the cargo office and called my boss in Columbus, Ohio and informed him of the problem. It was decided to wait until the next morning and fly a set of rollers in.

After I got off the phone the facility manager mentioned he had a stack of 8' long 2" diameter pipe out back and wondered if they would help. It worked for the Egyptians placing one log in front of the other. Why not me?

We grabbed the pipe and, after a couple hours of work, the generator and a few misc. crates were on the airplane and we were ready to fly. The call was made to headquarters to let dispatch know we were ready to go.

This earned me an ass chewing by the dispatcher who had cancelled flight plans and sent the flight crew to a hotel. He told me I should have notified him we were loading. I told him sorry, but I didn't know it would work until it worked. After a while plans were set, and we were off to the Canadian wilderness.

The cargo supervisor congratulated me on a job well done. As most of SATs flying was for the military and used aluminum sheets and roller floors, that was what most loadmasters were used to. After this incident I was known as their best "junk hauler." See what I mean about titles?

This worked out well for me because I was always being called out for all the odd flying jobs which popped up all the time. It helped me accumulate a lot of flying hours and a fairly regular paycheck. It also educated my new wife to what it was like to live with a "fly boy".

"Drive on's" which wheel and track vehicles of all kinds, shapes, and sizes were known as, were a major portion of our cargo hauling. They were, for the most part, a welcome change to fighting skids, crates, and

Conex's on and off the airplane. You simply lowered the Herc's ramp to the ground, added a couple of truck ramps to the end of the airplane and drove the vehicle on or off. Chaining them down usually wasn't bad although some vehicles were hard to find a place for the chains. Of course, if the vehicles had been playing in the mud and oil, I also had a chance to play in mud and oil.

Other items required very special equipment to transport, like fuel tanks for diesel fuel and gasoline. On the Electra, which I first started on, the tanks were bolted to the floor and all the plumbing attached. Fuel was almost all we hauled in those days. The exploratory drillings consumed great quantities of fuel to operate and stay warm. When you think of it, it was quite ironic; we consumed 3,000 gallons of fuel to haul them 4,000 gallons of fuel to use in their endeavor to find more fuel.

Two other items we hauled on the Electra to the North Slope were dynamite and Styrofoam. The dynamite I'll save for a later chapter, the Styrofoam was used under the permanent runways to help prevent frost heaves from forming. As the runways were 1-mile-long by 150' wide you can imagine the quantity of foam we hauled.

The fuel tanks for the Herc were built on 40' long skid/cart. The tanks were rolled in on rubber tires then the tires lifted up and everything chained to the floor. These tanks could hold 7,600 gallons though 7,200 gallons would bring us up to weight for most destinations in Alaska.

There were also special aluminum tanks built especially for transporting powder cement. The tanks were chained down in the Herc; a specially designed truck would back up to the cargo door and blow the cement through hoses into the tanks. Due to an accident before my time, cement became the easiest and most sought-after load for a loadmaster to haul.

The tanks were in and chained down when the Haliburton truck showed up with its load of powder cement. The truck backed up to the airplane and the foolish, energetic, and productive loadmaster that we all were, raced out to help the Haliburton crew drag in the hoses and hook them up to the tanks. The hookup fittings were new and different from anything he'd worked before, but he thought he had them hooked up right. Somewhere in the process of blowing the cement in, one of his fittings came loose and the Herc was promptly filled with very heavy cement. Also considered an error!

This resulted in some serious down time as the tanks had to be emptied, pulled back out, and the entire floor pulled up. Every nook and cranny had to be swept out and vacuumed to get the heavy powder out so the Herc could get back to its normal weight hauling capability.

After that, all the loadmaster was allowed to do on a Haliburton trip was to operate the switch that opened and closed the cargo door. Thus it was a lucky day when you were assigned to an airplane hauling cement. I also think it was a source of many bribes to the ramp supervisor.

The other cargo mostly hauled was pallets which were set on the ramp and we moved them into place with an electric battery powered pallet jack. This system was used on mail and scheduled freight to various villages in Alaska we supplied. This was also how we loaded and off-loaded auto parts, at times a major contract with our airplanes. The parts were picked up from different manufactures and hauled to assembly plants around the lower 48 and Mexico.

Back in Alaska, and away from the North Slope for a change, (Thank God), were the summer fish hauls. Salmon from Bristol Bay needed to get to the processors in Kenai and Anchorage and needed to get there now. It was an around the clock affair that lasted about a month.

After palletized freight we are down to the famous and highly overrated hand jib. In Alaska this consisted of stuffing plastic pipe, fiberglass insulation, furniture, and any small item that wouldn't fit on the skid. This was especially true if the destination was a Native village we rarely flew to.

Some loads were the whole list of building materials, appliances, food, and whatever else it took to build a house or lodge in a remote location. The customer wanted the total use of the expensive Herc he chartered, and hand jibbing was the only way to accomplish this.

When it comes to Africa, hand jibs where almost always the mode of operation. Only places like Nairobi would have the luxury of a forklift. Everywhere else it was the famous Congo line for loading and offloading. There was always plenty of manpower when we were hauling food and supplies to the refugee camps. I only had to do the tie down straps, which was about all I could handle in the oppressive jungle heat.

Not one to search out physical labor, I must have been feeling a little frisky that day at Kisangani in the middle of the Congo. I had untied the load and a Congo line of Africans had formed on both sides of the cargo compartment. They were about halfway done when I noticed a gap in one line so I jumped in. When the African turned to pass the bag of rice to his comrade and saw me, he dropped the bag on the floor with his jaw right behind it. I bent over, grabbed the bag, and handed it the next man in line while joining in on their chant. "Hi yah hi yah ye" I sang while passing bags. The line on the other side came to a halt when they saw me. I don't suppose another white man had ever been crazy enough to do something like that. Soon they picked the tempo back up and all were singing and laughing along with me. It almost killed me, but the look on their faces was worth it.

Flying as a loadmaster put me in many situations I would rather not be in, but mostly it let me see places this old farm boy never ever even dreamed of while I was growing up. While in Africa we flew each day over the place where they filmed the movie "Out of Africa." It was one of the most beautiful spots I've ever been. Farther west were both active and dead volcanoes in the middle of a big blue lake, then endless jungle where rivers could barely be seen due to the jungle canopy.

Spending most of my life and most of my flying time in Alaska, grand views of mountains and glaciers became commonplace. Even the magnificent Alps of Europe, while beautiful, were not impressive compared to Alaska. The big difference was that every valley in the Alps had a town or towns. In Alaska there might not be a village for hundreds of miles from the valley we were flying over.

While never close to the Himalaya's, the most impressive mountains I have seen are the Andes

Mountains of South America. There are rows of mountains taller than Mount McKinley.

This was never made clearer to me than the day we were flying from Rio de Janeiro to Santiago, Chile. We were flying along fat, dumb, and happy, when the flight engineer announced that with our cargo and fuel load, if we should lose an engine, we wouldn't be able to maintain enough altitude to clear the mountains that by now were all around us. Though we rarely lost an engine on the dependable Herc, it happens from time to time. This was a mandatory consideration when filing a flight plan. It seemed to me on the ground in Rio would have been a much better place to discover this fact.

The most interesting place this job took me to was Papua New Guinea. It was the year of the El Nino and one of the rainiest places on earth was having a drought. Normally supplies for this mine, employing thousands of local natives were barged up a river. The river had all but dried up and we were there for nine weeks flying in 7.5 million pounds of food and supplies to the mine.

A quarter of a mile trip from the town of Wewak, located on the north shore of PNG, would take us back a thousand years. The natives pretty much still lived the same. Grass huts, open cook fires, spearing fish, and bows and arrows were the norm. Just a little while before we arrived, a new tribe had been discovered for the first time. Flying over the jungle you could see different villages on ridge tops. At times they would still be at war with each other. Just 5 miles west of the mine we were flying to, the aviation maps were blank. The pages read; "No known data, highest elevation thought to be _____" the only other place I've run across this was areas in the headwaters of the Amazon River in South America.

As with any job, there are good days and bad days, duties you hated to do and those you liked.

Being a loadmaster was no different. In the early days, when I was flying for GNA and AIA, a good day was usually when I didn't have to work in -60° chill factors or colder, much colder.

After years of this work, mostly on the North Slope, I had no idea how good the job could really get. Good duty was issued by seniority. By the time I had earned any seniority, I was flying for Mark Air and they were phasing out the Hercs to become a big time passenger airline. My dreams of flying around the world like the stories I had heard were demolished, just like Mark Air's dreams of becoming a real airline.

A few years passed with me doing any job available, running heavy equipment mostly. One day Southern Air Transport (SAT) called and asked if I would like to go back flying. Their first offer on salary was a joke and I told them so, a while later they called back with a decent offer and I was back in aviation.

SAT flew all over the world and soon I was too. As my passport became filled with stamped pages I was amazed. I even had to get pages added to my passport long before it was to expire. After a few years of this flying, home became a place I got to visit once in a while, and I wondered what a good day on the job really was.

Well, I'll tell you.

MY favorite part of the job was known as an "engine haul". All of the major airlines sooner or later ended up with an airplane in some far-off place with a bad engine. Enter our Herc; it was the only aircraft other than 747 that a jet engine would fit on. The Herc was less expensive than a 747 to charter and was the first one called upon. The aircraft on the ground would cost the air carrier a million dollars a day in lost revenue. As you can imagine, they wanted a new engine and they wanted it now! Our salespeople of course knew this, so after settling on some super exorbitant rate, we were off.

We would first go to the air carrier's main base and load up. The load consisted of a new engine on a stand, a stand for the bad engine, elevated platforms for engine removal, and the tools, oils and odds and ends required for an engine swap.

Here's the good part. After loading up, we would head for our destination, such as Hawaii, Fiji, U.S. Virgin Islands, and Aruba among many other exotic places. After a long flight, (a Herc is not a fighter jet, it cruises at 275 knots) we would arrive and unload the engine and misc. parts.

Here's the better part. The engine swap would normally to be around 24 hours to complete and have the new engine running. Being in a far-off place, we would be forced to wait until the swap was done and haul the bad engine and tools back. This meant a whole day at a paradise most people only dream of coming to and getting paid for it. Some jobs, I swear!

That's pretty much the job. Now let's see what the hell we are hauling.

Did Someone Say, Outsized Loads

CHAPTER 2 - THE CARGO

No airplane that I ever knew of made any money for its owners flying around empty. That's what our sales departments were for, finding stuff to put in the airplane that needs to be somewhere else.

What did we haul? I don't know where to begin, but a wise man once said, "Start at the beginning." O.K. that's what I'll do.

My first flight as told in the introduction was as a tanker. We hauled diesel fuel and gasoline to the North Slope. Except for some Styrofoam and dynamite my first three winters were all hauling fuel.

The Lockheed Electra that GNA had, though originally built for passengers in the 1950's, made an excellent tanker. The tanks allowed plenty of room to move around and the pump system was run off from the airplanes hydraulic system. This was a safe, efficient system. We could land, pump off 4,200 gallons of fuel and take back off in less than 30 minutes. N404GN was the best set up tanker in Alaska.

We supplied exploratory drill rigs, cat trains, research labs and some villages with fuel. Ninety percent of our landings were on ice strips plowed out on nearby lakes. They weren't always smooth, but they were always hard to find in the vast whiteness of the artic, where all our destinations were.

In the spring of 1980 GNA was bought out by Alaska Int'l Air (AIA) and I moved over to the Herc operations. This was a whole new ball game and one I wanted to learn. With its vast cargo compartment, the things the Herc could haul was an endless list. I was getting tired of always smelling like diesel fuel anyway.

A lot of building materials were being moved out to the villages at this time. Lumber, roofing, windows, and tanks among many other things all went on a skid and into the airplane. Fire trucks, ambulances, and school buses, everything it took to upgrade the villages was flown in.

Oil rigs were constantly being moved and gold mines, as they expanded, needed newer and bigger equipment all of the time. The mighty Herc was capable of hauling a D-9 cat. It took 3 loads to accomplish this because of the weight. A D-6 cat, 966 loaders, a 14G road grader and excavators could usually be driven in whole with the removal of the cab for height clearances. It never ceased to amaze me, even years later, when I'd go in the back to have a smoke, I'd look at this huge chunk of yellow iron then look down out of the round porthole windows at the ground 4 miles below and say, "We're actually flying". We must be crazy.

By the time winter rolled around again I had long since been turned loose on my own to make it and hopefully not break it. The loadmasters training me could only show me so much and when they thought I was ready to learn the rest on my own, out I went. For the next twenty some years I kept right on learning. You were always coming across something you had never hauled before.

Winter meant the lakes were frozen up enough on the North Slope for exploratory oil drilling to begin. Seismic work was completed, and cat trains would head overland to positions where drilling was to begin.

A cat train consisted of a cat pulling a string of steel sleds 20 to 30 feet long and 8 to 10 feet wide. On the sleds were built cook shack, sleeping quarters, generator set, fuel tanks, and whatever else that was needed to accomplish the work and survive in Alaska's arctic. Usually crews of 3 or 4 men were on the train. This was not a job for the faint of heart, especially for the cat operator. More than one operator ended up at the bottom of a lake when he hit thin ice and went through with no time to escape. It was very disheartening to have a cup of coffee with a man one day only to fly in a few days later and find out he was at the bottom of a lake.

The cat train would find a large lake near the proposed drill site, set up camp and take the cat out and plow out an airstrip on the ice. A typical runway would be 1 mile long and 150 feet wide. Holes were drilled in the ice to measure the thickness. The Herc needed at least 36" of fresh water ice to land on. At times near the coast we would land on the ocean where we needed 48" of salt water ice.

Now the airlift could begin. A large off-loading ramp was plowed off and runway lights were laid out on the ice. For me this was the start of some of the hardest work I've ever done. Oil companies wanted a full airplane for the expensive charter rates. This meant loads of 45 to 50,000 pounds and if possible, all available space used. Drill rigs were broken down in pieces, the size and weight, which would fit in the airplane, supposedly. Ground crews seemed to think a ½" here and there didn't matter, but 1/16 of an inch matters. Don't forget that ice and oily dirt added thickness to the steel beams and platforms also.

While drill rigs were up and operational the workers had the habit of welding large bolts to the structures in handy spots to hang needed tools. Handy for them, but a nightmare for us poor, innocent loadmasters. The bolts were hard to see and would catch the sides of the airplane. The support stanchions in the tail were a popular target. This would cause me to write up a damage report, (more dreaded paperwork), and mechanics hours of work in the freezing cold. But they still loved me, at least I think they did, and they still let me keep my beer in their warm up shack.

The camp units, called ATCO units, were a necessary part of a rig move. These units housed generators, kitchens, bathrooms, bedrooms, and shops, everything they needed. I don't know who leaked out the dimensions of the Herc, but they should have been hanged for "high treason". The camp unit builders sure took them to heart. A unit would stretch from cockpit to tail, floor to ceiling, and wall to wall with ½" clearance all around. This required them to be winched in on the plywood floor with no rollers and be perfectly aligned to the airplane before even starting. If you happened to be an oil worker missing the door handle to your bedroom, I'm sure I know nothing about it.

The easiest loads of course, were the "drive on's," pick-ups, suburban's, and trucks. Huge fuel tanks, cones, small out buildings, dumpsters, and a huge array of odds and ends completed the picture. All in all, a "rig move" took around 200 trips. This wasn't counting the drilling mud, fuel, food, and other supplies in constant need. A "rig move" was a huge undertaking, throw in 24 hours of darkness, the -60° ambient temperature, the minus 100° chill factors, blowing snow, and slippery ice, you might begin to get an idea of what it was like, but I doubt it. Unless you were actually there doing it, whether working the ground, or the air, most people would never believe what these operations entailed.

Heavy equipment was something the Herc was constantly called upon to transport. It was the only airplane in commercial use that the equipment would fit in. Mining ventures and construction companies required many pieces of equipment at remote job sites. A lot of pieces were a simple drive on, but some need a good coat of Vaseline to slide in. Putting large pieces of equipment onboard was slow hazardous work and very stressful for the loadmaster and operator alike. The operator had to make small, smooth movements as the piece was slowly driven in and out of the airplane. All the while the loadmaster was crawling around tight places checking for clearance making sure the airplane wasn't hit. In the battle of steel equipment versus the aluminum airplane, the airplane was always the expensive loser.

This would cause the loadmaster much paperwork and severe weight loss from the boss's ass chewing.

One time a construction company out of Fairbanks had a remote project going where, among other equipment, they needed three huge rock trucks. With tires 5 feet tall and weighing in at 46,000 pounds they were a sizeable load. Being almost as wide as the cargo hold and a foot too tall, some adjustments had to be made. The exhaust stacks and a few other objects on top were unbolted, now it was down to where we thought by letting air out of the tires it would go in.

The rock trucks were hauled out on a low deck trailer which was backed up to the Herc and we began to back the truck into the airplane. Things went fine until we reached the center section. This is where the wings cross over the fuselage and is the main thing that restricts the height of a load. The underside of the wings has a slight curve to them and brings the distance down to the protective plywood floor to exactly 9 feet.

The monstrous dump box was about 2" too tall, no problem, we'd let the air out of the four huge tires on the back axles. This was done while I kept checking the clearance. Finally, we were down to where the dump box would clear with a little room to spare. A little clearance under the wing section was nice. Hitting the underside of the wing was a bigger sin than selling your sister on a street corner! "Back it up slow" the driver was told... Whoa! Whoa! Now that we had clearance under the wing, the tires had flattened out too wide to go between the walls.

The walls in the center section were vertical, not curved out like the rest of the fuselage, to store the main landing gear in flight. Ah (four letter word) now what? Well we called a local truck tire shop to come out with an air compressor to put some air back in the tires. We finally pumped them up like "Goldilocks bed," not too hard, not too soft, just right, and after 3 ½ hours we were ready, one down and two to go.

The second truck we were careful not to let too much air out of the tires and had it loaded in 1 ½ hours. While loading this one I noticed a 1 ½" block of steel between the dump box and the truck frame. The questioned mechanic said yes, it could come off and should have been thought of before.

Before the third truck was brought out those blocks were removed, and we had the truck on in 45 minutes. They say, "practice makes perfect," not in my case, but it did show I was teachable.

Fish hauls took up a big chunk of time in the summer and were almost considered a vacation after the winter rig moves. Three or four Hercs would leave Fairbanks for Kenai, AK to haul salmon from Bristol Bay to the fish processors in Kenai or Anchorage.

The fish were stacked with ice in a 4x4x3 high plastic fish tote and weighed about a ton each. The totes were placed on the ramp with a small forklift and we would distribute them on the airplane with an electric pallet jack. Sounds easy enough, well it was, and it wasn't.

The totes were so loaded down with fish that their tails hung over the sides and the lids were loosely thrown on top. When you flew through rough air the fish slime would slop out on the floor making it as slippery as an ice skating rink. Then the pallet jack became a real challenge to steer and would lose traction, so we'd have to push on it for all we were worth. I'm sure there were times I looked like a novice figure skater.

Tying down was another matter, as you threw straps over the totes and hooked them to the floor rings, the fish tails would rub all over you. The fish, still alive, would slap you in the face. After a shift I smelled so much like a salmon, if I swam up river all the female fish would have gathered around me like a rock star!

Why the cab drivers would give us a ride to the hotel, I'll never know. One morning after a rough night of flying, I paid the cab driver and a generous tip and turned and entered the hotel lobby. It was 7am and the lobby was packed with Japanese tourists waiting to board the tour buses. I headed for the elevator and the people parted like the Red Sea. It was just another episode. After entering my hotel room, I took off my boots, and walking right into the shower.

Such was fish hauling, but remember, this was a vacation!

Hauling auto parts to assembly plants kept us very busy at times. Most auto parts are hauled by train or truck, being a much cheaper form of transportation. We only flew in case of a shortage at the plant. I was told one time that it cost $60,000 a minute to shut down an assembly plant while it was running. Yet you would be surprised how much quantity we flew. It wasn't unheard of to have a Leer jet chartered to fly a box of bolts. We once flew a load of 300 plastic gas tanks to Mexico for a charter price of $75,000. Figure that out in the price per car.

Hauling auto parts was mostly pretty easy and mundane. The occasional load of complete truck frames and the very heavy racks of pickup truck axles were anything but easy. Most auto parts were in wire baskets that fit right into the assembly line upon arrival. They also had the added bonus of no fish tails to slap you in the face.

So much for the normal stuff, let's get on to the exotic, unique, mystifying, and unheard of ...ah, hell, it's all just cargo.

While I was employed at Southern Air Transport they were called upon to haul a famous "star". "Keiko," the killer whale of movie fame needed to be moved. If you saw any news coverage of this, it showed a C-130 Herc with a UPS logo on the tail. In reality it was a SAT Herc with a SAT flight crew that did the job. UPS paid for and used it as advertisement.

I got you going, I'm sorry to say it wasn't me on that famous flight, but I did haul a live whale once. We picked it up in Chicago and flew it to New Hampshire someplace, so it could mate with another whale. This, I'm sure, was more expensive than a New York Governors call girl.

Though it wasn't "Keiko", there was still a large gathering of people and TV news cameras there as we prepared to load up the water tank and whale. There were professors, biologists, doctors, veterinarians, and there must have been a few lawyers too. Each one was more important than the other. You could tell by the 14 people giving the poor truck driver directions as he backed up to the airplane. Common sense would tell you no man can watch 14 people at once and follow their directions. I've found through life, in the highly educated, sense isn't "common."

When the truck and trailer were nearing the airplane, I went out to talk to the driver, informing him to just watch this ol' hippy and things would turn out fine. When I returned to the airplane people were piling bags of ice on the ramp. "Where do you want this? It's to keep the water at a certain temperature. Common sense and a lazy loadmaster would have winched the tank in first and stacked the ton of ice behind. Since they all wanted something to do and the ice was in the way already, I had them carry it to the front of the cargo compartment where it was warmer and would melt faster.

The tank and whale were winched in with two guys in wet suits in the tank to keep the whale calm. They remained there the whole flight.

Arrival in New Hampshire was met with the same fanfare. It must have been some special female whale he was flying to see. For all that, they only used a few bags of ice to keep him cool. Me, I would have needed the whole ton.

The only other time I can remember news cameras on the scene was in Houston and Dallas in 1985. We were called on by the Red Cross to fly emergency supplies to Mexico City after the devastating earthquake. Our first trip was the important one. We flew television news teams, satellite dishes and equipment in so you too, could enjoy the devastation. Getting down to business, the second trip was stuffed to capacity with blankets, bandages, water, light plants, and generators. We flew for five days along with every available aircraft at the time.

The airport in Mexico City, by our second trip, was a madhouse as we taxied in. Airplanes from our Herc to giant 747's where everywhere being off loaded with ground crews frantically trying to keep up. It was my first trip to a third world county and I learned a couple of things.

The very first things to come off our Herc were two light plants weighing 2,000 pounds apiece. I was informed no forklifts would be available for a long time. My inquiry of how we would get them off was answered by 40 Mexicans walking in, picking up the plants and carried them off. Showed me, stupid Gringo! The rest of the cargo was carried out in short order.

When I first went to the back of the Herc to open the ramp and door, I opened a new pack of cigarettes, pulled one out, lit it, and set the pack on the ramp control box. After the load was off and everybody gone I decided a cigarette would taste good while I shut the door, I picked up the pack which was still there, but there wasn't one cigarette left inside!

Oh, by the way, neither with the whale or the Mexico City trips did I ever find out if I made the editors cut on the news film and was aired on T.V. I doubt it, Hollywood hasn't called yet.

An oil rig fire north of Dawson City in Canada sent us on an urgent flight to Elk City, OK in the mid 1980's. We were there to fly all the firefighting equipment for the famous "Red Adair" team that they would need to put the fire out. It was 110° in Elk City at the time and the inside of the Herc on the black asphalt ramp was like an oven. This longtime Alaskan passed out twice while loading, coming to flat on my back on the floor with a circle of Okies looking down and telling me I should slow down.

Another oddity along oilfield lines was a deep-sea diving bell we picked up at JFK and flew it to Newfoundland where they needed it for under water work on an offshore drill rig. It was my first time at JFK and the immensity of that airport was astonishing. The tower knew we were lost the minute he read Alaska Int'l Air on the side of the Herc. They sent out a "follow me" truck to lead us to the cargo outfit some five or six taxi miles away.

The generator wasn't very big. It only took up one of the eight sections in the cargo compartment. It wasn't a full load weight wise, but at 35,000 pounds it was close, and once in the airplane it was like trying to tie down a bowling ball in a shoe box. The generator had failed in Caracas, Venezuela and needed to go back to Italy for warranty work. With the right ground handling equipment, it would have been an easy load, with what they had, it was a nightmare.

The generator showed up on a large flatbed truck, behind it came one of the largest cranes I have ever seen. They had planned to just pick it up off from the truck and set it in the airplane, only one catch I could see, an airplane has a roof on it. As always, my lack of knowledge of any foreign language was a huge barrier. Through hand gestures I figured out that they intended to pick it up and extend the boom into the airplane and set it on the floor, OK!? Through hand gestures I indicated to them that the generator was 4 feet high, the huge hook was 3 feet high, the block was 4 feet in diameter, the crane boom was 4 feet thick and the hole in the back of the airplane was only 9 feet high. Oh!

A little 4-wheel cart was found that was used for normal cargo containers and the generator was set on it. I thought the wheels would collapse, but they didn't, they waited until it was pushed up behind the airplane, then all 4-wheels collapsed. Now the generator and the sheet of aluminum it was setting on was almost a foot lower than the thickness of my rollers and ramp which was lowered to the ground. It was going to be one of those days.

After what seemed like a week two small fork lifts showed up. Both together weren't strong enough to lift the cart and generator. After another week, one slightly bigger forklift was found, still not able to lift the whole cart. We were finally able to at least lift the end toward the airplane. You haven't a clue as to how many hand gestures all this took, and they did keep using this one hand gesture to me that was easily translated in any language.

I got everything hooked up and we winched the generator partially onto the ramp. To decrease the incline of the pull I lifted the ramp, which brought the nose wheels of the airplane 6 feet off of the ground. This act always brought the cameras out as crew members took pictures of each other under the wheels holding up a whole airplane.

Well we got the generator on and I used every cargo strap there was and a couple of chains to hold the roly-poly nightmare in place, then it was off to Italy and a well-deserved pizza.

Another generator piece was one of the biggest oddities I've hauled. The piece was the armature shaft, just the shaft, and it weighed 46,000 pounds. It was going from Santo Domingo back to Texas to be rebuilt, as it was the only one like it in the world. I won't go into the gory details on this one, other than to say it showed up after a 4 hour wait down in the valley of a low boy trailer rather than a level low deck trailer and it took 4 hours to put the blankety blank thing on the airplane.

Africa had its own off the wall cargo. I mentioned earlier about hauling food for the refugee camps, we also hauled the refugees themselves and all their belongings. While I personally never had that kind of load, I watched another Herc and loadmaster perform this operation.

They'd open up the ramp and the people, dogs, hogs, goats, chickens, and their few belongings would walk on, find a piece of floor and sit down. No first class or beverage cart on these flights. The mess after each one of these flights would do justice to Noah's Ark, but it accomplished the task of saving lives and moved many people out of harm's way in a hurry.

This same operation could have been used after Katrina, needing only a small length of dry road. Wouldn't you much rather have a sore ass from sitting on a floor for a while than standing in water up to your chin. Of course, we all know now the government's response to the devastation of Katrina. After years of dealing with military and government charters on our Hercs, I could have told you, and I'm telling you now. Do not rely on our government dysfunctional operations during and after a disaster, help yourself!

We flew a few other loads to various countries in Africa, but I can't remember the details. I do have a photo at home from one African load. It shows a rickety wooden crate being shoved into the airplane by a group of Africans Sticking out of the top of the crate you can see the necks and heads of 3 baby giraffes. They were being transferred to a game refuge. They were beautiful and smart enough to duck their heads.

Over in Europe we picked up the job as a feeder airline for the huge KLM cargo airline. We were based in Amsterdam and flew cargo to some of the smaller cities around Europe. The Herc was set up with a roller deck floor and cargo was put on aluminum sheets which fit between two side rails and are held down by locks built right in the floor. This is the way most cargo aircraft in the world are set up, but for us Alaska Herc jerks this was something new.

The cargo was, as you can imagine, a misc. assortment of goods you buy in your local shopping mall, but there was a couple of notable exceptions I'd like to tell you about.

Lintz, Austria was one of the cities on our list, surrounded by farm land, farming supplies were usually a large portion of the cargo headed there. One night as the KLM ground handlers brought out our load, I could hear very slightly a strange sound mostly drowned out by the loud airport noise. As we were loading up a look into the containers showed we had a whole airplane load of baby chicks. Once inside the airplane and through the entire flight they all but drowned out the noise of the four engines. They didn't even flap their tiny wings to help out on fuel consumption, they just went "peep, peep, peep" all the way home.

If I was going to load up an airplane with chicks, it would have been the tall, blonde and beautiful ones we would see going through the KLM flight attendant offices and lounge on the way out to our airplane. Nobody ever asks my opinions on anything!

The other load I'll always remember was one out of Amsterdam to Ireland. Most of the load was regular freight, but part of it was two aluminum pallets hooked together and a corral built around the edges. Inside were two of the most beautiful horses I've ever had the chance to see. They were race horses worth a million bucks a piece and the trainer was right there in the corral with them. The lady who owned the horses was already up in the cockpit, seatbelt on and ready to go wherever those horses were going.

Everything was going fine and dandy until the flight engineer came back to tell the trainer he had to come up to the flight deck and buckle up for taxiing and take off.

The trainer in broken English informed the engineer there was no way in hell he was going to leave the horses. The engineer insisted, equally as hard the trainer insisted. What to do? Ah, this was a job for the captain.

So, the engineer went up to the cockpit and brought the captain back. The captain told the trainer he needed to come to the cockpit and put a seatbelt on, it was FAA rules. The trainer, no more impressed with four bars than two said "Hell no. I won't go!" Now what? I sure as hell didn't want to unload the whole airplane and start over again, so I decided it was time I put my two cents worth in.

Pointing up to the control cables which, on a Herc are suspended below the ceiling out of the way of the cargo, but still hanging out in the open I caught the captain's attention. "Don't you think you'd rather stay in control of the airplane rather than an excited rearing up horse with no pilot's license" I said. Besides the FAA is a long way from here." The captain turned to the engineer and said, "let's crank 'em up", and off they went to begin our flight. Just another day on the job.

It Fit, Barely!

Back in Alaska there wasn't much "exotic stuff" hauled. An occasional hot piece for the Prudhoe Bay oilfields would send us on a rush trip to Texas and back to the North Slope. I did however one time haul a whole dog team, sled and all, back to Anchorage from Nome after the famed Iditarod dog race. Don't know who the musher knew to have this happen, but I'll bet the dogs were happy not to be stuffed in their kennels. Kinda like flying first class even though I didn't' serve them any Champagne.

During the years I was flying on the Electra for GNA, my later good friend and boss for many years, Jim Wilde flew a circus to the Eskimo village of Barrow on a Herc. Before he became the great boss he was, he was a lowly loadmaster. Wait a minute, he's not my boss now. I don't have to butter him up!

The circus was flown up for the entertainment of the Eskimo school kids who had never seen anything like that before, hell they've never even seen a tree before. Of course, the whole circus wouldn't fit in a Herc, but they took what they could, including a 10,000-pound elephant. Jim made sure the elephant was tied down good and couldn't move. An elephant walking around in an airplane would sure raise havoc with the C.G.

Another Herc was sent up later that day to bring the circus back to Fairbanks. Tim Bailey was the loadmaster on that trip. He told me they didn't have any problems except that when the elephant felt the heat coming from the opening Herc door he wanted on now, but he had to wait his turn to be in the center of the airplane.

So much for cargo, oh wait, I promised you a bear story. You can't write an Alaskan book without a bear story, it's against the law.

Once upon a time in the vast reaches of the North Slope, near the town of Deadhorse lived a great bear. This was no ordinary bear for he wanted to abolish all aircraft from landing at night at the Deadhorse airstrip.

Actually, quite a few grizzly bears have lived around the oilfields for years, drawn in by the smell of cooking T-Bones and dumpsters full of waste food. To my knowledge only one bear had to be put down, he was a great bear, the largest tundra grizzly ever seen. A big, beautiful bear, "Tobi" as he came to be called, co-habited with the oilfield workers for many years. His downfall was finally wanting his own room in the Prudhoe Bay Hotel and was shot in the hallway. It was a very sad day in Deadhorse, for all the people knew and loved "Tobi."

Meanwhile back to the villain of this story. He was a normal sized bear wandering the tundra and streets of Deadhorse. Boredom overtook him because he invented the game of "Bat the light." Every night he would walk along the edge of the runway and knock out the runway lights, going from one to the next. The Department of Transportation figured he did around $10,000 worth of damage a night, something had to be done so Fish and Game was called in.

They caught up with the bear one night and darted him with a tranquilizer. He was then loaded up on a truck headed down the Haul road. They took him about 150 miles and turned him loose in the Brooks Range. Three nights later he was back to continue with his games and Fish and Game was called again.

It just so happened at that time we were in Deadhorse engaged in a rig move to a spot near Point Lay on Alaska's west coast. After he was darted they put him on our airplane and we flew him 400 miles to his new home. He must have figured the game wasn't fun enough for that long of a journey, for he never came back.

CHAPTER 3 - THE AIRPLANES

While Wilbur and Orville didn't haul anything, it wasn't too many years after that the usefulness of an airplane to get cargo to remote sites became evident. In Alaska airplanes put dog teams hauling freight and the mail out of business. As airplanes became bigger and better the payloads became bigger. Today 747's can haul more than half a million pounds and the huge Russian Antonov is capable of hauling more than that.

Most cargo airplanes started out in the military, but as they were phased out for better equipment they went into use for commercial applications. Airplanes were bought, companies were started, and cargo aviation became a boom or bust operation. Not so more than in

Alaska where few roads and unending wilderness made airplanes the only way to supply outlying villages, mines, and of course oilfields. The book "Triumph Over Turbulence" written by Jim Magoffin, founder and owner of Interior Airways, later Alaska Int'l Air, tells the story of hauling freight to the North Slope. It tells of the escalation of the size of cargo and the airplanes needed to accomplish this. It is an excellent read.

Best Tanker in Alaska

The older cargo airplanes were before my time, so I can't tell you much about them. They say to write what you know, that leaves me with the Lockheed Electra and the C-130 Hercules.

Working part time for Omni Logistics, a ground handler based at Fairbanks Int'l Airport, owned and operated by my longtime friend and another poor creature who "had to be my boss" Burnie Hall, I had the chance to load some of the older cargo airplanes. Over the years we've handled DC-3's, DC-4s, DC-6s, C-46s, Skyvans, Cossas, and airplanes all the way up to 747s and the Antonovs, the largest cargo planes in the world.

Load mastering on the Electra's I've pretty much covered. Originally built in the early 1950's as the state of the art passenger airplane, it started out with a few minor flaws, such as the wings vibrating until they fell off. The Electra had a relatively short production run as we stepped into the Jet Age with the introduction of the Boeing 707. The flaw was fixed, and the Electra became a useful and very dependable aircraft. Though there are very few flying in commercial use today, the military still uses them quite a bit under the nomenclature P-3 Orion.

This brings us to the C-130 Hercules, arguably the best workhorse ever built. Today the new C-17 is taking away some of the long time Herc duties. I believe even for military purposes the Herc will never go out of demand. Commercially the C-17 is way too expensive so the venerable Herc will always have a job.

The A model Herc first came out in 1954. Over the years it has been improved upon and with a short suspension is still being produced as a J model. This makes it the longest running production of any airplane in history and shows what a remarkably useful airplane it is.

The commercial Hercs I flew on were dubbed the L-382 or C-130-30. They were a double stretched version of the stubby military C-130s you see so often on the TV news. With an eight-foot section added both in front and behind the wings, the 16-foot longer cargo compartment was much more versatile for commercial use.

S.A.T. had a single stretch, or -20 Herc based in Africa and was the only one I ever saw. The stretch was put in forward of the wings with none in the tail. This led to a fun experience in Nairobi, Kenya where we were flying food to refugee camps in the Congo.

I had no experience loading a Herc in this configuration and was always worried about getting it too nose heavy too fly. It was hard to judge the volume of food bags and where to start piling it in the front of the cargo compartment. A few times I started a little far back which led to problems at the tail end of the load. On this trip I looked outside at what was left and realized we would have to stack the 100-pound sacks a lot higher to keep from being tail heavy.

When the next bag was placed at my feet I flexed my arm, patted my bicep, and pointed to the nearest African, indicating by movements we need to throw the bag up on top and was he strong enough. He grabbed his end of the bag and on 3 up it went. My end of the bag made it, his didn't. Immediately his comrades started to razz him, and I joined in. As the next young man in line stepped up I made great fanfare of flexing my muscle. Through motions I asked if he was sure he was tough enough. The game was on and we all had great fun until the load was finished. I couldn't speak their language, nor they mine, but we still made fun of hard work.

The L-382's cargo compartment was 53 feet long from winch to ramp hinge, 10 feet wide and 9 feet high at both the center section and door entrance. Herc load planners were drawn up and given to customers to plan their loads accordingly. Sometimes all of us loadmasters hated those planners because the customer would fill up the space with no thought of how we could move it there. An example, the rollers we needed underneath were 3 1/4" high, now we were down to 8 feet 8 1/2 inches, not the 9 feet as advertised. Ten-foot-wide meant 10-foot-wide, not 10 foot 1/8 inch. Actually, some clearance was needed, so 9' 11 7/8" was sometimes put in the airplane. Regarding length, if you think 53 feet would give you room to play with, you'd be wrong. I was amazed at how many times we would be down to a 1/4 of an inch clearance as to whether we could shut the door or not.

Tying down the load so it didn't move was the most critical part of any venture. This was done using metal rings in the floor. Along each side of the cargo compartment were 7 large rings rated at 25,000 pounds tensile strength and were the most used. In between these rings and spaced all throughout the floor were small rings rated at 10,000 pounds tensile strength. The ribs on the fuselage wall had rings rated at 5,000 pounds tensile strength. Even with all these rings it was sometimes hard to find a way to tie an object down.

Along with the rings were chains with a special curved hook on one end that had the same rating as the floor rings. The hook end would be wrapped around a beam, axle, frame, or any solid spot you could find on an object and hooked to the chain. On the other end of the chain went a device called, well, a device. The device was hooked to a floor ring, you pulled the chain as tight as you could and slid a chain link into a slot in the device and cam over a lock tab. To finish tightening you turned a knurl nut on threads until tight.

Sounds easy, but until you were good at it you did a lot of turning on the knurl nut. I found this out the first week I worked on the Herc as the rookie I was. My forearms became so sore; to brush my teeth I held the brush in my hand and shook my head.

One of the things that made the Herc such a versatile airplane was the ability to fly with the rear ramp and door open. Air drops became a big feature for the Herc, with the military dropping paratroopers, supplies, and jeeps. Even a Sheridan tank could be hooked to parachutes and pulled out the back.

This feature was also used in commercial applications. Food drops for the Int'l Red Cross were carried out in Africa wherever airstrips weren't available, or a landing was too dangerous. The loadmasters wore a harness around the upper body. A strap with a hook on the end was measured out to the end of the ramp and hooked to a floor ring for safety. Going out the back door with the load could put a serious crimp in your vacation plans.

Back in Alaska there was only one operation that required open door flying. I do recall a couple of flights with roof trusses that were flown to a village at low level with the door open because of over length. The main operation was for Alyeska Pipeline and was a spraying operation in response to an oil spill on water. I took one practice run on it, and it was my first experience working with the door open. The scariest part was deploying the spray arms out to each side of the airplane. You had to walk out to the very corner of the ramp to swing the arms out and lock in place. Meanwhile the 150-mph wind was trying to blow your feet out from under you. The most recent use of this system was in the Gulf of Mexico after that oilrig explosion.

Another open-door experience is one I have to relate because as far as I know, it's the only time it's ever been done. The auto manufacturer Renault of France contacted Lynden Air Cargo (LAC) to see if we would air drop some cars for a TV commercial they wanted to shoot. The idea was tossed around for a while and it was decided to give it a try. I'm glad they did; as I was called on to participate in this unique operation.

Much preparation was needed to get this operation rolling. First off, a location was needed to pull off this stunt and it had to be a large area with nothing around. Right off the bat the FAA prohibited it from happening anywhere over American soil. Now I'm sure they used their finest dartboard in coming to this decision. A spot in the Mexican desert south of Yuma, Arizona was chosen. With my taste for paperwork, I'm glad I wasn't involved in the amount of red tape there must have been.

LAC's cargo manager, Jerry Stout, went down to Mexico a few days early to make preparations for the big event. Three old Ford Taurus's all the same color were found and made ready for the air drop. The first problem was easy to foresee, as soon as the rear tires cleared the ramp on the way out, the car would fall on its frame and stop. The solution was to weld box steel tubing under the cars frame. We would chain down some of the afore mentioned rollers as close to the end of the ramp as possible for the box steel tubes to roll out on. This was a good plan and worked well when we pushed the cars out. The rest of the plans.... not so good.

A Hollywood stunt director was hired; the film company's director and producer, our cargo manager, and who knows who else were all in on making the plans for the air drop. I wasn't there at the time all of the plans were made and changed and changed again, but I'll do my best to describe what happened.

From the beginning they wanted the cars to glide to the ground and not tumble like it would going off a cliff. The first step was to strip the cars of their engines, transmissions, and all extra pieces like mirrors, and wipers, etc. For this they hired some locals who gladly had at it as they also would be able to keep the parts.

The next item on the list was to balance the cars. This was accomplished by setting a car on a fulcrum point and sand bags were added in the trunk. So far, so good. Now it was decided a little aerodynamics was needed on the underside of the car. This was done by painting some plywood black and metal band it to the underside of the car.

Now for some reason, don't ask me, it was determined the tires and wheels should come off and just slide the cars out on the box steel and rollers. Okay, all almost agreed. The tires and wheels came off, but not the normal easy way. They took an acetylene torch and cut off the spindles and axles, you'll see later why this fact is important. Should be ready to go now. Wrong!

Now the director and producer decide that they just don't look like a real car without the tires and wheels. Very observant! By now it's too late to find more cars so the cut off spindles tires and wheels are found and welded back on the cars. Finally, ready.

The next day, enter stage right, we show up with the Herc and the Leer Jet that's filming the whole operation makes its appearance. What a beautiful airplane it was, it's the one that shoots the US Air Force commercials you see on T.V. The rest of the day was spent chaining the rollers down and making final preparations. Checking and rechecking, but mostly trying to survive the 120° temperature.

That night after dinner was the big meeting with everybody to lay out the plans, duties, and communications for a successful shoot. We had three cars and three attempts to succeed. Communications were necessary between our Herc, the Leer Jet, and the ground crew. We also had to lay out plans between the cockpit and Jerry and I in the cargo compartment.

Actually, we didn't have that much to do. The pilot, Mike Remond, would call over the headsets "20 seconds out", which would cue Jerry and I to turn on the movie cameras mounted up by the ceiling to film the car going out the door. Then we would get to the front of the car ready to push it out when Mike said, "drop zone". We'd push the car out and turn off the cameras until the next attempt. "Out of the drop zone" would be the last we heard for each attempt. We could handle that, after all, we were going to be movie stars.

The next morning everybody was up, had breakfast and headed out to the small airport where the action was to get underway. Jerry and I put on our technician's outfit, for that was the starring role we played in the commercial. We were starting the process of loading the cars when the director noticed our white tennis shoes. This would not do as the footage shot in France had technicians with black shoes "Wardrobe!" A nice looking young French gal showed up, soon found some black tape and proceeded to cover our shoes with it. Jerry and I were already too good looking to need make-up.

Back to work, one car was loaded on a car hauler truck and backed up to the airplane. We pushed the car onto the ramp and jostled it around to make sure the box steel lined up with the rollers. OK let's push it to the front of the airplane. We started pushing and hadn't gone 15 feet when the car was into the wall of the airplane. Remember the weld job? It wasn't straight and there was no steering now. Not OK. Out the car went and another one brought up. This one went straight enough to work and the other two were put on with the crooked one last. Back in business.

The next puzzle was how to tie the cars down. The chains wouldn't work because the hook end always got hung up in the undercarriage of the car and we wouldn't have the time to undo them. We decided to just throw straps over them, one around the front windshield, and one around the rear windshield. After all we weren't going to land with them onboard.

This still left us with the problem of holding the car ready to go out the door in place until we were ready to push it out. Neither a chain nor a strap would work because of the time factor. We were going to have to be pretty quick to hit the drop zone. Jerry said, "I know, we'll use a rope just like we did with the horse back home on the ranch." We found a length of strong rope, tied it to the car and Jerry ran the rope to a wall ring to show me how it works. He tied the rope to the ring using a bowline knot I think, stood back, looked at it, stepped forward, grabbed the slack end and gave it a tug. The knot came loose, and the rope fell to the floor. "Good idea Jerry, no wonder you're the boss" I said. Now our part in the venture was all set to go. I even had my hair combed to cover the bald spot, move over Kevin Costner here I come.

Soon everybody was ready, we closed the ramp and door, taxied out, and took off. Jerry and I put on our safety harnesses, donned our headsets and waited to hear from the pilot. It was a short flight to the drop zone and the excitement was building. In a little bit Mike's voice came over the headset saying we were almost there and that he had slowed down enough to open the door. Jerry opened the door and the ramp came down. I walked back to the edge of the ramp and the end of my harness strap to have a look around. Behind us and to our left was the

Leer Jet. As I looked down to the sandy desert I could see the ground crew and their vehicles, waiting. Three or four vehicles were visible from our altitude of 500 feet buried nose first in the sand. They were for props I assumed.

"Okay we'll make a big circle and come back over for the first drop" Mike told us over the headset, "get ready". This was it! I unloosened the straps leaving the rear one loosely in place to keep the car from going out of the door onto someone's farmhouse. We pushed the car into place on the ramp. Jerry tied the rope to a floor ring, real good for use on all three cars. He then tied his famous bowline knot to the car's bumper. I finished taking the rear strap off and we're ready for "action".

Slowly we completed the big circle and lined up on the drop zone, the Leer Jet was behind us ready to shoot. Jerry and I waited in eager anticipation of the 20 second warning call. All of a sudden over the headset came "5 seconds!" The look on Jerry's face must have mirrored my own, was that 5 seconds from the warning call or 5 seconds from the drop zone? An excited voice on the headset saying "drop zone" answered that question.

Jerry and I stood there with blank looks. "Out of drop zone" startled us both back to reality. In a little bit Mike asks, "How did it go guys?" Jerry says "Wweee...ittt...yyyou..., the car is still here, what happened to our 20 second warning call?" "Sorry we were a little busy up here, we'll do better next pass."

I'm sure they were busy up there, the 123° heat wave and a wind had us bouncing around until we could hardly stand there in the back. Mike had to keep the airplane around 500 feet off the ground, slow enough so we didn't rip the ramp off yet fast enough that the speedy Leer Jet didn't stall, all the while communicating with everyone involved.

Around we go until we were lined up with the drop zone again. Jerry and I were listening for our calls, eager to get the car out this time. "Twenty seconds" blares in our ears, we rush back to turn our cameras on and get to the front of the car ready to push it out. Jerry grabs the slack end of the rope, we're ready! "Drop zone" rings loud and clear, I'm ready to push, Jerry tugs on the rope, nothing, he yanks harder, still nothing. Jerry puts one foot on the car for more leverage and pulls and yanks, nothing, he switches feet and tugs for all he's worth, still nothing. I swear, though I don't know how he did it, he had both feet on the bumper, yanking on the rope with all his strength, still nothing. "Out of drop zone" snaps through our headsets and Jerry, mad as a hornet by now, keeps tugging for at least another 5 seconds still to no avail.

Now Jerry is a very large man, the sight of him dancing around and bracing himself one way then another, all the while yanking on the rope, was more than I could stand. I had long since been rolling around the floor in uncontrollable laughter gasping for air. I finally got myself together enough to remember the cameras needed to be turned off or they would run out of film. "Jerry, the cameras" I yelled. You could see the heat waves coming off his head through the heat waves coming off the desert. We both managed to get our cameras turned off and I went back to holding my sides and laughing. Jerry went back to fuming, which made me laugh all the harder.

"Well guys, how did that one go, better?" Mike asked. His query was answered with total silence on our part, finally one of us said, "We couldn't get the car out, it's still here." We explained what had happened as we continued our circle for another pass. The rough air had bounced the car up and down until the knot had become so tight there was no undoing it.

By now, I'm sure, the Leer Jet crew and the ground crew are wondering what the hell is going on. Two passes and nothing tangible accomplished. What kind of outfit did they hire? I'll have to admit, up until then we hadn't looked too good!

Third times the charm, right? I pulled out my trusty Leatherman to cut the rope and we were ready. This time, one way or another, that damn car was going out! Even if I had to drive it!

The headsets roared "20 seconds," okay, cameras turned on, knife ready, "drop zone," a slash of the knife, a handy push, and out went the car. Success! Sort of.

When the car went out the door I quickly turned the camera off and went to the end of the ramp to watch. When the car hit the 150-mph air, the rear windshield blew out, the trunk popped open, one tire fell off, and the sheets of plywood underneath were ripped off.

All in all, it looked like we had thrown a small junkyard out the back door. I'm sure this wasn't the footage the director had in mind.

Jerry and I hustled to get the next car in place on the ramp while we circled around. We put it in place, tied it down with the "trusty rope," grabbed my Leatherman and were ready just in time for the next drop.

This one went off without a hitch. Once out of the door the car glided down with no parts flying off and looked good all the way down until I saw a cloud of sand and dust. As we were getting the third car ready, Mike's voice came over the headset "you won't believe it guys, that one stuck in the sand nose first almost in line with the others." War hoops could be heard all around, Jerry and I included. About that time and halfway to the ramp with the third car, the passenger side front tire and wheel fell off. We would have pushed it out anyway, but with the frame on the floor, we couldn't budge it. So much for the afore mentioned weld job.

We let Mike know what had happened and a discussion was taken to the radio. It was decided we would go back and land, pull the car out, weld the wheel back on and go back up for a third try. While on the ground getting the car repaired the director had a chance to review the footage shot from the Leer Jet. The first one was of course, a flop, but the second run was declared perfect. We couldn't have done it any better, so the third run was scrapped, and we were out of "show biz!"

Everyone involved was promised a tape of the completed commercial. A month later we received our tapes. I couldn't wait to slip it in the VCR. What the...? Jerry and I weren't even on it, in fact, after all the time and preparation, the Herc was only on for two seconds, long enough to see the car come out the back. Hollywood still hasn't called.

There's one other airplane I would like to mention in this chapter, that's the C-133. Two of them are sitting at the Anchorage Int'l Airport. One was for parts and one that flew, the only one in the world that can be flown. Known as "The Widow Maker" for its reputation of coming apart in mid-air, it was decommissioned and prohibited from flying years ago.

I had a chance to go all through this airplane when it was in Galena, Alaska, flying into the Illinois Creek goldmine. We were there with a Herc and flew 95% of the equipment and supplies in. The C-133 flew a dozen trips with equipment that was too large or too heavy for the Herc. We moved unbelievable equipment on this operation, things that weren't even tried on the oil pipeline.

Being prohibited to fly, the FAA fined the owner $5,000 each time it took off. This was, of course, just tacked on to the charter bill the customer received. Kudos to anyone who would fly an airplane known as "The Widow Maker" and kudos to the FAA for their paper chasing ability.

A few years back someone at the FAA, excelling at his job, was reading through the Jeppson manuals that cover Alaska. It was discovered that quite a few airstrips, a lot of them military, contained the words "go around impossible" in the description of the runway. It was decided they couldn't have that in the manual, it sounded unsafe. The words were changed to read "go around improbable" in the newer editions.

They changed the words but didn't move the mountains at the end of the runways that was still impossible to go through. It's the government, as long as the paperwork is right, actual things don't matter.

The airplanes loaded and ready, who's driving this bus anyway?

Getting Ready to Offload

CHAPTER 4 - THE PEOPLE

I n aviation, as in all walks of life, you run into all kinds of people; some whom you will never forget, some that were a joy to work with, and some who you wonder why they are allowed oxygen. Flying around the world put me in contact with many different cultures and people. The job of loadmaster required working mostly with flight crew members and ground handlers. Occasionally there were the contractors, project managers, and the customers who had chartered the Herc. From multi-millionaires to the loin-clothed natives and all standings in life in between, this job brought you in contact with all of them. It was my job to keep them happy with the service the airline I was working for at the time provided.

They say to save the best until last but being the hippy rebel I am that's not going to happen. As I stated in the introduction, my first night of flying as a loadmaster was with the best. The night I started, I didn't even qualify as a rookie, the pilot, "Jorgy" already qualified as a legend. By this time, he had many years in aviation and many hours behind the yoke. When Jorgy sat down in that left seat, he put that airplane on him like you and I would put on a suit. When he was flying no matter what happened, you knew you were coming home at the end of the shift. I sometimes doubted that old Electra, who wouldn't. I sometimes counted as much as 36 DMI (deferred maintenance item) stickers plastered around the cockpit, but I never doubted Jorgy.

No matter where we were flying he'd look down and say, "see where that river forks, the hill to the left, I was charged by a grizzly there." Or "see that gnarly mountain? We shot a real nice Dall sheep there once." "That lake down there, had to put a plane down on it once." Hearing his stories always added pleasure to a trip and relieved the boredom. One of his favorite past times on the North Slope was to get clearance from Anchorage center to go VFR, as he reached to pull the throttles back for decent, he would turn and say, "let's go wolf hunting." The fact we spotted an artic fox on the snow-covered tundra one time, speaks of how close he liked to get to his "work".

When he was flying, in his flight bag would be 5 different pairs of glasses, each one a different color for varying light and weather conditions. As we were approaching an airstrip, he'd say to me, "Dig out the pair of glasses in the red case for me, would you?" "Sure." I'd look through them, and sure enough. They would improve your ability to see out of the windshield. One other thing he always did, and he was the only pilot I ever saw do this, was to leave all of the interior lights on at night during takeoff. "You don't need to see out, but if we have an emergency we need to find control buttons, breakers, and levers in here, and fast. Made sense to me!

I could write a whole chapter on Jorgy. I spent more hours flying with him than any other pilot that I can think of, but I won't because he has his own book out now titled, "Jorgy." Find a copy, it's very worthwhile reading and I'll have a couple of Jorgy stories in a later chapter.

A few years back they held a big dinner party to celebrate Jorgy's 80th birthday. It was the best big affair I've ever attended. With all the people who've known Jorgy over the years it was necessary to make it an invitation only affair. There were many long-time pilots, airline owners, and dignitaries of all kinds, hundreds of people. Of these only four loadmasters were there, Jim Wilde, Al Holmberg, Terry Paz, and myself. It's the biggest feather I'll ever have in my hat and if it sounds like I'm bragging, it's because I am!

Jim Branham was another pilot from the Electra days. Another man who had stories from the expanses of Alaska passing below us and we enjoyed our times in that old airplane. Not so for some of the crew members. Known as "The Rock" because of his serious, nothing but the best job attitude, Jim expected the best from himself and his crew. In a job where one mistake could be your last, I didn't see anything wrong with his demeanor. He admonished me one night, but only 'cause it was my fault and I had it coming.

The long hours of flying fuel were catching up to me. When you hook up the hoses to pump fuel you need to open the correct valves for the tanks and open the air valve which vented all of the tanks to the outside of the airplane. With fuel coming in the air needs to go out, and heaven forbid you should overfill a tank; the fuel would spray outside and not fill the airplane.

One night I had hooked up the hose and motioned to the fueler to start pumping. I double checked the tank valves with my flashlight. Everything was fine as I fought to fully awaken from the short nap I had on the return flight. After a while strange creaking noises seemed to be coming from everywhere in the airplane. Something was wrong! Shining my flashlight around, I suddenly remembered the air valve! I shined my light on the valve, sure enough, it was shut, oh no! Leaping to the valve located over one of the tanks I pulled on the handle, I pulled harder, there was too much pressure on it and it wouldn't budge. Now what? Something needed to be done and done fast. I could run to the open door in front of the fuselage and yell to the fueler to shut the pump off, but what if he wasn't near the switch? I jumped up on the tank and bracing my feet against the fuselage I pulled for all I was worth. The valve slid open with an explosive whoosh!

I'm sure the people in Delta Junction, a hundred miles away, didn't know what that sound was that night when they heard it, but anyone around the fuel pit did. Jim flew out of the cockpit door yelling "damn it, you have to open the "bleeping" air valve." Looking back, I can't remember if that happened in a month I had 230 hours of flight time or just 220 hours. Sorry Jim.

Years later in the bone yard I've seen tanks caved in and blown apart. I've heard of airplanes accidentally filled with fuel and not in the tanks or wings.

Over the years I flew with hundreds of pilots and crew members. We had a good working relationship. I depended on them to not crash and kill me, they depended on me not to let the cargo break loose and kill them. Remember we usually had 46,000 pounds behind us sitting on rollers.

I'd have to say 90% of the pilots were good people of varying levels of skill, the rest...not so good. I could fill pages of boring stories about the good people, but that's no fun, so let's pick on the rest for a while.

In my early days on the Herc a lot of time was spent on the cold, windy North Slope. One load we were picking up one day was extremely tough. The skid was coated in frost and ice and was very heavy. It had been sitting on the huge sled for a long time and was frozen down. The minus 50° temperature wasn't helping matters either. After 1 ½ hours of hard work and frustration it was finally in the airplane and I was chaining it down. While knelt down working feverishly on a device, I noticed a pair of boots in front of me, then I heard, in a smart ass voice, "What the hell is taking so long?" When I looked up I don't know if it was the sweat running off my face or the look in my eyes that gave it away, but this man was already making tracks for the cockpit. He made it up the steps to the flight deck before I was able to get a hold of him, his lucky day.

This man was an excellent pilot who had devised many helpful methods for navigation and in finding runways during a white out. As a person, he was just too full of himself. I probably shouldn't have done that, but you just don't ask a man sweating at -50° that question.

In all my years of flying only one other captain received my "complete attention." He was a retired colonel from the Air Force and treated people like a high uppity officer would. He ordered the crew around and threated the mechanic and I like buck privates. This had been going on for a week or so as we jaunted around the globe and was getting pretty old. We had reached our final destination for the day and were shutting down and preparing to go to the hotel. The captain came down the flight deck stairs, stepped into the cargo compartment, pointed in the corner at his suitcase and ordered me to carry it out to the waiting courtesy van. Many times, at the end of the day if I didn't have anything to do at that destination, I would haul all of the baggage out to the van while the crew finished off the logbook and paperwork. It was a courtesy and speeded up getting to the hotel and a good shower.

Being the "mild mannered reporter" that I am, I grabbed the front of his shirt and ever so gently placed him against the bulkhead wall. He was then informed that he was not in the military anymore, that I never had been, and if he talked to me that way one more time I would rearrange his face. For the rest of those trips and on future trips, he never talked down to me nor did I ever hear him order a crew member around. It just pays to have good manners.

In the old days on the North Slope the only thing to look forward to at the end of a hard day's work was a good hot meal. Now days some facilities have weight rooms, gyms, even swimming pools, but before that the meal was the high light of the day.

It was always nice to drop in to a rig camp at mealtime. This meant while I was offloading the Herc and putting the backhaul on, the flight crew would get a ride to the mess hall, sit down and eat a hot meal, then fill a Styrofoam container and bring me back a hot meal. This beat the hell out of a cold sandwich that we seemed to always live on. Most crews that is.

The crew had just returned from their meal as I closed up the door and tightened a few things down. I headed for the cockpit in anticipation of a rare hot meal.

I climbed the ladder to the cockpit and looked around for my meal. No meal. This wasn't the first time this had happened with this crew. Hitting the engineer on the shoulder, I asked "where's my food?" No answer, they wouldn't even look back at me. By this time all four engines were running, I walked down the steps, out the crew door, and over to the same Suburban that had given them a ride. He took me to the mess hall where first a cup of coffee and a cigarette seemed in order, then a salad, now the meal, and then another coffee and cigarette. We drove back to the airplane where I thanked the driver for his patience.

When I got back onboard the airplane not a word was said. They cranked engines and back to work we went. This was the kind of crew that thought so little of a loadmaster; they didn't even enter his name in the log book.

On the other end of the ladder, and the upper end I might add, were captains like Rollin Broughton, one of a few retired military pilots worth a damn. We were in Galena, Alaska along the mighty Yukon River, hauling equipment to a goldmine south of there. Lunch time had rolled around and while I was busy putting a load on, Rollin walked a quarter of a mile to the lodge we were staying at. He ate his lunch and walked back with lunches for the mechanic and me. This was no easy feat. The grass field and woods he walked through were infested with a zillion hungry mosquitos. Along the Yukon they were huge mosquitos, I've seen some with "N" numbers.

Somethings just get to you, the way somebody does something, or the lengths they go to. One thing that got to me while flying was the crew briefing on the "before landing checklist". This was done on every landing and the captain would give the crew briefing. Most times, by most pilots, it was a normal reading. "We'll be landing on runway 12, if we have a missed approach we'll go to heading such and such and go around, any problem will be treated as an inflight emergency." It might entail a couple other items, but that was pretty much it.

Enter captain "Worry Wart" and after the engineer said "crew briefing" you'd hear something like this. "We'll be landing from the south, that's because we're headed north. If we should miss the approach we'll pull up, fly around, and decide whether the cargo is important enough to try landing again. Should we lose #1 engine we'll fly to the left due to the lack of power on that side. If we have a fire in #2 engine, the engineer will run back out on the wing and piss on it. A #3 engine loss will have the co-pilot filling his underwear while the engineer holds his nose. Should #4 engine even stutter, I want the co-pilot and loadmaster to grab their left nut and lean to the right."

By this time, if we haven't already overshot the runway, we're close, and if we did have an actual emergency, the crew would have been so confused, the only thing they would have been able to do, was write Ann Landers.

The best crew briefing was from longtime co-worker and friend, Ray Peters. Ray started out as a loadmaster, took engineer training, then pilot training, and was a co-pilot when I met him. With his skills, it wasn't long before he was a captain. I've spent more time flying with him than most other captains and the before landing briefing was always the same. After "crew briefing" was called out, Ray would say "were going to roar in there and land" which is exactly what we did.

Ray had another flying habit I was fond of and that was the way he would land. The touchdown was almost always smooth which he would follow with reversing the props before the nose wheels were on the ground. This would give me a chill up and down my spine like a good old song would. It felt right, and I would love to have some film of this taken from somebody on the ground.

This action was deemed unsafe by most pilots and procedure manuals. The nose wheel was supposed to be on the ground before reversing props in case a prop hung up going into reverse. The number of people with more landings in a C-130 than me can be counted on one hand. I've never been on board when this has happened nor have I talked to anyone who has had this happen. Oh well, they say "shit happens," they also say, "if it feels good, do it."

So much for "The Good, the Bad", let's get on to "The Ugly." For the most part, us loadmasters were hard working, hard drinking, and short on sleeping all around good guys. Being each out on his own flying most of the time, we didn't work together that much. Sometimes at the start of a shift there could be four Hercs waiting to be loaded, so 5 or 6 of us would hit each airplane and "Git RR Done.!"

This would mean 5 or 6 different ways to get the job done. It was long ago decided the man assigned that airplane was "the boss." Unless he asked for an opinion, he wasn't supposed to get one. Did I say that?

When we weren't flying we would work in the yard with the yard hands building the many, many loads that kept the Hercs flying. It would be both a change of pace and a relief not to have to fly once in a while. Some loadmasters, after years of flying, preferred to work the yard. Working the yard required us to be proficient as an equipment operator, mostly fork lift experience. We always said, to be a loadmaster, you had to be an operator, teamster, laborer, and being half monkey didn't hurt either.

AIA had 7 Hercs when I started work there, down from the 13 they had during the Alaska pipeline boom.

There were around 25 loadmasters to man the 7 Hercs around the clock and we were still shorthanded at times. This was due in part to people always being on the injured list. It was a dangerous job and injuries were frequent. Ranging from sprained backs and torn muscles, to broken bones, and the usual cuts and bruises, it was rare when the list had no names on it. Breaking winch cables and chains, along with falls and nearly being crushed were common occurrences. Let's not forget frostbite, heat stroke and being overcome by exhaust fumes. It was a job you needed to pay attention to at all times and try to foresee accidents in the making.

One incident on the North Slope comes to mind. The loadmaster was back unhooking chains from the load as the airplane was taxing to ramp parking at a drill rig site. The airplane had stopped so he undid one of the last two chains that still held the load in place on the rollers. For some reason the crew then taxied ahead to another parking spot which caused the load to move. The loadmaster was in the center section where the quarters are tight. As the load moved he was rolled sideways between the load and the wall. With both shoulders separated and stuck fast he could only yell for help.

The flight crew heard him and ran back to see what was wrong. The crew hooked up the winch to move the load, but as this would have caused him more pain, he yelled for them to not do this. The crew, at a loss as to what to do, noticed another Herc taxing in, and went over to get the loadmaster from it. The loadmaster came over and hooked up a chain to the load in such a way that would have moved the load away from the injured man as it was winched ahead. This worked out and the man was soon free and flown back to Fairbanks for medical attention.

A loadmaster was judged not only by how little damage occurred to the airplane on his watch, but also how quick his turn around times were. This was especially true from the flight crews who were paid only when the airplane was moving, known as block time.

Taking off chains while taxing was a common practice and to my knowledge the previous story was the only time something happened We'd usually have all but two chains off, one to keep the load from going forward, one to keep it from rolling backward, and the rear door open by the time we were parked. Then a ramp block was placed under the ramp for support and a bumper board put on the end of the ramp for the truck and trailer to back up against. A good ground crew would already be backing up the trailer and the winch cable would be strung out ready to be hooked to the load.

In this way we could sometimes land, taxi in, pull the 48,000-pound load off, taxi out and be taking off in less than 10 minutes. Very impressive! This took teamwork from a good loadmaster and a very good and well-trained ground crew. Some of these ground crews had worked together for years loading and unloading Hercs and it showed. They have my deepest gratitude for making my job easier and for me spending less time freezing my ass off. I got along well with all the ground crews I worked with on the North Slope. One exception was the truck driver who came at me swinging a chain binder, him...not so well.

One secret to shorter ground times was making sure everything was straight and lined up as best you could before you even started loading or offloading. A little bit off was a lot off by the time the load moved 60 feet and moving 24 ton around wasn't easy. Most loads were lined up fairly easy and unless the skid was twisted, or the ground was uneven went straight in. I don't know what it was about some loads, a crooked stack of lumber on the skid, the way the light hit it or what, but some loads were as hard to line up straight as finding the English words on a package these days.

None of us loadmasters were perfect; we made mistakes, from minor airplane damage, to major airplane damage. Overloading the airplane was a distinct possibility due to there being no scales at remote sites. We carried a list of some known weights but making a hopefully good guess was the only option a lot of times. I know planes were overloaded at times and it is a tribute to the mighty Herc for always making it off the ground.

I've heard of one fatal crash due to a loadmaster's mistake. This was a DC-8 out of Miami a few years ago. The airplane took off and all of the cargo went to the rear of the airplane making it too tail heavy to fly. The loadmasters with this airline did not fly with the airplane or I guarantee he would have done a much more conscientious job.

One of the popular ways a Herc would get overloaded was with dump trucks. Usually two tandem axle dump trucks could be hauled at a time, making it roughly a 40 to 45,000-pound load. This left room to add some more weight. Some customers seemed to think if you put it in the dump box it didn't make the load heavier. Oil and fuel drums, tool boxes, generators, anything could be in the box and it paid to check it out. I was warned of this early in my career and always looked in the boxes.

A friend of mine learned the hard way. They flew into a construction site to move equipment to a new job site. One of the loads was two dump trucks which he had the drivers drive on and he chained them down. Nothing was said about cargo in the dump boxes nor did he check. Taxiing to the end of the airstrip, they turned around and took off. Reaching the other end of the runway they couldn't get airborne. They pulled back on the yoke and desperately tried to fly. Putting the landing gear up to reduce drag they managed to stay airborne and slowly climbed out. Turning to the loadmaster in unison, the crew's faces said "What the hell's going on?"

The loadmaster went back to do his after-takeoff check. While he was in the back he looked in each dump box. To his horror he found a D-8 cat track rolled up in each truck box. This would have made the Herc at least 12,000 pounds' overweight. I reckon Hercules was a god.

The other severely overloaded Herc I know about was hauling fish. Years back the fishing industry had smaller fish totes made, obviously you had to put more of these on for a full load. The numbers were pretty well set for each load, but somehow this load the numbers were mixed up. The Herc ended up being loaded with regular totes but at the small tote number. An educated guess on my part would put the load 18 to 20,000 pounds overweight.

The only thing that saved the day was that they were flying out of King Salmon, Alaska. It was a major fishing port for Bristol Bay. It was also a military airstrip and was 10,000 feet long. Why takeoff wasn't aborted I don't know. They used the whole runway and were able to stay airborne by closing up the landing gear reducing drag. They made it back to Anchorage but, I heard later, blueberry bushes were found snagged in the landing gear doors. Blueberry bushes do not grow very tall.

I had one experience I remember dealing with an overweight load. It wasn't drastically overweight like the last two instances, but we were heavy, maybe 6 or 7,000 pounds. The soft dirt runway didn't help matters either.

Yantarni Bay is located on the southern coast of the Alaska Peninsula south of Becharof Lake. Chevron had a test hole drill rig located there and it was time to pull it out. The load for that trip was sections of drill stem pipe, something we've hauled many loads of. As I started to winch the skid load off from the trailer I noticed it was pulling harder than normal. Stopping to check the skid condition out nothing could be found wrong. I finished winching it in until the airplane was balanced, but before I chained it down I wanted to have the captain to check it out. He had been flying Hercs many years hauling oilfield supplies and I wanted his opinion.

"Oh yeah, we can handle this no problem" was the confident reply. "Okay, but I'm letting you know I think its heavy," I added. I chained the load down and yelled "crank em up." As I took my seat in the cockpit we were taxiing to the end of the runway. I noticed we went out into the scrub brush as far as we dared before turning around. Now comes the part my simple mind never could agree with. For short field take off the procedures manual, Lockheed, and the military recommend you stop, lock up the brakes, run the engines up to full power, release the brakes, and take off. As I and any uneducated Appalachian hillbilly will tell you from experience, that anything moving a little is easier to get going than something at a standstill. Alaskan bush pilots also agree on this.

Around we came and stopped facing down the runway, which ended in a 400-foot sheer cliff to the ocean below. Usually when you release the brakes on this type of takeoff the airplane jumps a few feet and then rolls out. The engines were wound to full power, the airplane was vibrating like a cheap hotel bed, off came the brakes and...nothing happened! Finally, we started rolling slowly in the soft dirt, slowly we picked up speed, slowly the air speed indicator climbed, slowly we began moving faster, and there was no runway left to abort anyway. "V-R rotate," the captain pulled back on the yoke and...nothing happened! Now everybody became concerned, the pilot pushed hard on the power levers looking for all the power we could get. There was very little runway left and the cliff was fast approaching. Damn! I hadn't brought my swim trunks. Again, the pilot pulled back on the yoke and the nose wheels grudgingly lifted off the runway. The main gear was still on the ground and to this day I believe it stayed there until we went over the cliff.

I thought that with no ground effect ahead we would be sinking but, the mighty Herc roared off toward the clouds and not the water. As we climbed out, the captain and co-pilot turned to me with their arms extended, palms up and going up and down. Sure...now he thinks it's heavy. I was busy ignoring them as I was in desperate need of removing some seat fabric from the crack of my ass. I've thought about that load many times since and I believe the drill stem sections were longer than what we've normally hauled.

Having the load or parts of the load break loose on landing happened to loadmasters once in a while. So, let's get my bad out of the way before we move on to bigger and worse things.

The load was a normal load except for two 40' long pieces of plastic pipe 5-6" in diameter and fairly thick walled. We put them on last, sliding them over the top of the skid load and I strapped them down. I even put 2x4s in the holes up front and belly wrapped straps around the wood to hold them in place. After takeoff I went back and retightened everything, double checking the pipe.

During the long flight to Barrow the vibrations and settling of cargo loosened the pipe enough to allow them to slide back and the 2x4s fell out unheard over the engine noise. We descended and landed on the runway, when the pilot reversed the props and hit the brakes, the two pieces of pipe slid forward hitting the back of the cockpit wall. Bang! They sounded like a stick of dynamite went off and needless to say, scared the hell out of us.

They pipe hit the fuel dipstick which was stored there breaking it into pieces. No other damage was done except maybe to our tickers.

I roared up behind the Herc as it taxied across the ramp to the far parking spot protected from the prop blast by the loaders windshield. "Turn em and burn em" was the motto for quick turnaround. It soon became apparent that this Herc wasn't going anywhere for a while. As I pulled up and looked in the back of the airplane I noticed the stack of 4 empty skids was setting awfully far forward in the cargo compartment. I climbed down out of the loader and jumped in the airplane for a look. The skids had broken loose on landing and were partially through the cockpit wall. The chains and devices were still hanging on the skids but had come loose from the floor rings.

There was only one explanation for this incident, the tired loadmaster had not gone back and retightened the forward restraints after the takeoff. While not damaging the elevated cockpit the 12,000-pound stack of skids took out a quarter of a million dollars' worth of radio and navigation equipment located under the cockpit. It was a very sad and sickening sight and a good friend and loadmaster lost his job that night.

The worst accident due to a lost load on a Herc I've heard of happened on a SAT Herc somewhere in Africa. Two dump trucks were the culprit again. Actually, an ex-military loadmaster was the culprit for an insufficient tie down job. While landing on a short, rough, unimproved runway the props were reversed and the brakes hit hard to stop in time. Both trucks broke free from insufficient tie down and went forward. Everyone would have been killed if not for this Herc having a 9G safety net installed. The net did its job which was to restrain a loose load with a strength 9 times the load weight. Upon impact the net attached to rings on the floor, ceiling, and walls would pull in collapsing the fuselage and letting the cockpit break loose and stay ahead of the load. This is precisely what happened and is why the flight crew survived.

The following incident concerning a lost load involved me somewhat. No wait, it's not what you think, I was the good guy here. Why else do you think I'd write about it?

We had been jaunting around South America for a week dropping off supplies for the American embassy located in various countries. On our way home, we stopped in Panama City for fuel and an overnight crew rest. While taxiing into parking we noticed another SAT Herc sitting on the ramp. While motoring by we noticed a big gaping hole in the rear cargo door.

Arriving at the hotel we ran into the other flight crew, minus the loadmaster, waiting for us. Now the whole story came out. The day before, they had stopped in Panama City to load up and head to South America. Part of the load was a Chevy van and was the last thing put on. As they were taking off they heard and felt a terrible crash. Feeling the plane tilt back, they aborted takeoff. The van came loose, went back up the ramp, hit the ramp block stored there and pushed it through the cargo door. This tore out cross members and ripped loose aluminum causing the large hole we had seen.

The plan from SAT headquarters was to put the load on the airplane that I was on and head back to South America. Damn! Remember me saying home was a place you only were able to visit? The next day I put the load on and because the flight crew I had been with was timed out they were to fly the broken airplane to Marietta, GA for repairs. The other crew and I headed south.

Everything was going along fine until the co-pilot asked me for the weight and balance sheet. I knew that would catch up to me one day. During S.A.T.s orientation class I was the only one of eight or ten loadmasters that wasn't ex-military and I had hardly ever seen this form. It was either filled out by the dispatch department or the co-pilot when out in the field at the three airlines I had formerly flown for. When the instructor held up the form in class for the next lesson, everybody went ya,ya,ya, we know all about that. I didn't raise my hand not wanting to appear more of a dunce than I already did being the only one not wearing a suit and tie, instead wearing my "Alaska suit" of Levi's and flannel shirt.

I handed the co-pilot a weight and balance sheet, he looked at it and said, "It's blank."

I could tell right off he was very perceptive. "I know, I don't know how to fill one out" was my reply."

"What kind of loadmaster doesn't know how to fill out a weight and balance form?", he asked in a smart-ass voice only a co-pilot can come up with. "The kind that doesn't let a van go out the back door on takeoff" I replied.

The captain who I knew from ground handling SAT Hercs in Alaska was a damn good pilot and knew my credentials. He was doubled up in laughter and instead of the ass chewing I thought was coming he pointed to the co-pilot and said, "You fill it out!"

Loadmaster stories could go on all night, just attend a loadmasters party, you'll see! Better bring your own beer though, there won't be any left.

Ground handlers for the most part were people you didn't get to know well unless it was a longtime project. One guy comes to mind down in Ypsilanti, Michigan. "Hawkeye" worked for Active Aerio Services at the Willow Run airport. They mostly handled auto parts for charters to auto assembly plants. Lynden Air Cargo had a contract with them for 1 or 2 Hercs for a couple of years. He remembered me from hauling a few loads out of there nearly 20 years prior to this contract. We became fast friends, both being avid woodworkers and traded exotic wood. I would bring down diamond willow from Alaska to trade for maple and walnut that I couldn't afford to buy in Alaska.

On the other end of the spectrum would be a guy like the one in a village south of Barrow, Alaska.

He would not watch my directions from his seat in the large 966 loader. One day while he was picking up a pallet off from the ramp the loaders rack hooked underneath the edge of the Hercs door opening. Not watching me, he lifted up lifting the airplane as well. At any moment he was going to break the main support for the tail of the airplane doing a conservative half million dollars' worth of damage. I grabbed a handy chain binder and threw it at the metal wall below his windshield. This had the desired effect of getting his attention. After having him lower his forks and backing away, I climbed up to the cab of the loader where a one-sided discussion ensued with a lot of four lettered "good manners."

The following day I was summoned to the boss's office, a frequent occurrence on my part. He had heard from the village council about the previous night's festivities. Strangely their version left out the part about the loader but spent a lot of time on the "good manners." After hearing my side of the story, the boss thanked me for saving the airplane and informed me I was no longer welcome in that village. You can't please all the people all the time.

Fortunately, this was a rare occurrence and most loading and offloading operations went smoothly as far as people were concerned.

Customers were on the same scale and were mostly decent people, especially when I remembered to remember, "The customer is always right." Their goal was to have their goods moved as efficiently as possible. A Herc charter was a very expensive part of any project and they wanted their money's worth. I didn't blame them.

Having a company representative there as loads were being built helped out immensely, especially when it came to priorities. That is, unless he didn't change his mind 4 times while you were building a load, or worse, change it after you had it all done. Sometimes help wasn't help at all.

One day we were headed back to Fairbanks after dropping a load off at the village of Venetie, Alaska when the engineer turned and hit me on the knee. "We're going to San Francisco" he said, "Sure we are?!" Well we were! An "engine haul" had come up and an airline needed a jet engine in Hawaii now.

In Fairbanks I ran home, packed a bag, and left the wife a note. "Gone to Hawaii, be back?"

Hours later we were taxiing to parking in San Francisco and it was turning into a 20 some hour day. When I opened the cargo door people started climbing up the ramp, each one dressed in a business suit, introduced himself, handed me a business card, and told me what he was in charge of. As they hung around I busied myself getting things ready to load the engine. Soon we were ready. A half hour later all I had was 5 business cards in my pocket and no engine showing up. We were tired, and a hotel room was looking good.

"Where's the engine?" I inquired of the group. "Oh, it's on the other side of the airport, they're bringing it over" was the answer. "Oh, who's in charge of that?" No one knew. Blessed are they who travel in circles, for they shall be called "Big Wheels."

Last, but certainly not least were the Natives, Aborigines, Indians, and Eskimos I worked with on my Herc travels. The chance to be a small part in their lives was the times I remember and cherish the most. They weren't fake, they weren't out to impress me as a lot of people do, they were themselves and I enjoyed every minute I spent with them.

Let's start like Johnny Horton wrote in his song "A way up north to Alaska." It's where I spent most of my time anyway. With Alaska's oil money in the state coffers, rebuilding the Eskimo villages became a priority and we have been to almost all of them. Never saw an igloo as that's only a myth, they were only used in an emergency to escape a raging storm. Never saw a polar bear though we spent hours flying over the Arctic Ocean ice looking for them, only to land at a village and hear "should have been here ten minutes ago, there was a polar bear right there."

It was in early May the year we were stationed in Barrow flying diesel fuel over to the village of Wainwright. For almost 3 weeks we emptied the huge storage tanks in Barrow to make room for the barge load of fuel arriving that summer. At that time there was no runway at Wainwright, so we were landing on the Arctic Ocean ice just on the edge of town.

It was right in the middle of whaling season and the hunters of Wainwright had killed a very large whale up the coast toward Barrow, near the Wiley Post, Will Rogers monument. It's where these two crashed their airplane and perished many years ago. The whale was close to 60 feet long and tremendously heavy. At this time a construction company was there building the airstrip now in use. They sent down a loader and a cat to help the villagers pull the huge whale up onto the shore ice so they could begin the job of butchering up the whale.

For days after we dropped off the load of fuel and while empty on the return trip we would buzz over the site of the kill. It was amazing how fast the huge whale disappeared. As we sat on the ice pumping off fuel sled loads of meat and blubber pulled by snow machines would go by. It was a wild time and the whole village was celebrating. I was glad to have a chance to see this and wished like hell I had a camera.

While the whale was being transported to town a group of 8 to 10-year-old boys were waiting on the ice for the return of the snow machines. Each day they ventured nearer to the airplane. At first, they held off a good distance, but each trip they became braver and came closer. The next trip they were about 50 feet from the plane playing football. I went out and got the ball and started throwing them passes while I worked my way back to the airplane to keep an eye on things. The next trip they were ready for me to play with them and were getting right up to the airplane. The next trip, you guessed it, when I wasn't looking some of them were in the airplane. I had to put my foot down then, but we went on playing football almost every day.

Wainwright turned out to be the best place to buy whale baleen and I purchased several pieces over the years. In all Eskimo villages the arrival of the Herc was a chance to sell their ivory carvings. Some were out of this world beautiful and I always wished I had more cash with me to buy rare pieces you didn't see in gift stores.

The interior native village all had short, rough runways, and by air was almost the only way to get there. The airstrip would accommodate single and twin-engine airplanes and an occasional DC-3 or DC-6.

Oil money was upgrading the villages at this time. Contractors would fly in to set things up and we would fly in the equipment and building materials needed for the job. They would let the natives know a big, big airplane would soon be flying in. We would roar in and land on the first trip and as we taxied to parking you could see the whole village had turned out. The ramp was lined with ATVs, snow machines, and people waving and cheering.

You could tell they were impressed when the 46,000-pound load of lumber for their new school came out the back door. After a few trips the excitement wore off and less people showed up. The first trip though, would always make us feel like celebrities. Hey, ya gotta take what you can get!

The Aborigines of Papua New Guinea were the most unique race of people I met in my travels. Well behind the advancements of our modern world, the mining and business ventures of the Australians were their only contact with the rest of the world for years. In 1997 when I was there more schooling had become available and it was obvious the children were more educated than their parents.

I arrived in the coastal town of Wewak almost a week before the Herc arrived to help get things organized for the seven million pounds of supplies we were to fly to a mine in the interior mountains.

One morning when the mining company's project manager showed up at the hotel to show us around he had his right-hand man, a native, with him. As we loaded up the double cab pickup, the native exited the truck so I could get in. I told him to stay inside and that

I would ride in the pick-up box. He gives me a funny look, so I assured him it was too hot for this Alaskan and that I would prefer the wind in the open box. He crawled in, I jumped in the back and off we went. I started to notice the looks we were getting a quarter of the way through town. The sight of a black native in the cab and a white man in the box must have been quite a cultural shock. The farther we went, the taller the native sat up in his seat.

The warehouse we were working out of had an office added off to one side. Just outside the office in the warehouse was a large refrigerator. One day the manager asked the native to get him some ice for his drink. When I saw the native with the ice tray in his hand I saw a chance to impart my vast knowledge and some Alaskan culture to him.

I walked up to him and while tapping the ice and pointing out the door at the visible ocean said to him "in Alaska the whole ocean turns to ice." Just then a big flatbed truck drove into view, "We can drive big trucks on the ocean "I relayed. The look he gave me told me much more than the broken pigeon English ever could, "Ya, and you drive big rocks around in your head!"

Snorkeling was a favorite pastime on our days off, the water and sea life were much better than any I've seen in Hawaii. Some days some of us would walk the mile back to the hotel leaving the truck for those who wanted to stay longer. We walked the beach where we could, but sometimes had to detour around a lagoon bringing us close to a small native village. As we walked around a little side bay, which, by the way still held Japanese concrete machine gun nests from World War II, we came upon a woman with a little 3 or 4-year-old girl at her side. We said "hi" and started to walk past. The pilot walked past, but as I walked past the little girl started screaming bloody murder and hid behind her mother's skirt.

I had noticed on days we went down to the open market place that the flight crew always held back letting me walk ahead. One day they finally told me why. They had noticed the small children hiding behind the tables and the strange looks the older natives directed toward me as I walked by. It was the crew's source of entertainment. Obviously, the man with the all-white hair was some sort of bad juju. I don't know, but it went a long way toward boosting my inferiority complex.

Deep in the heart of the African jungle was another interesting spot to meet people, though not under the best circumstances. When we were in places like that it was at the request of the International Red Cross hauling supplies to the refugee camps. Though the Red Cross workers went a long way toward hiding us from the atrocities and plight of the local natives, it was painfully obvious as to the devastating problems these people had.

One trip after we had offloaded the food and supplies, I noticed a 7 or 8-year-old girl standing behind the makeshift fence around the gravel ramp. On a whim I pulled out a little plastic bottle of ice-cold water from our cooler and walked over to her. Unscrewing the cap, I handed the shy back stepping girl the bottle and watched her for a few seconds. After I received a happy, gracious smile I headed back to the airplane. After a few steps I turned to watch her. Already a grown man had sneaked out of the jungle and was trying to wrestle the water bottle from her. As she desperately held on I raced back leaping the fence and scared the attacker off. I remained there until she was about done with the water before I returned to the airplane. I never looked back, I didn't want to see.

Many worldwide cargo carriers operated on these refugee supply runs. Among them was a Russian outfit flying their IL-76 cargo jets. The airplane, equipped with two huge engines, was capable of hauling over 80,000 pounds.

On this day the small gravel ramp was crowded with 4 airplanes at the same time. We had just finished offloading and the IL-76 was cranking engines for departure. They started taxiing toward the runway with engines roaring way beyond needed power in an all fire hurry. When they turned toward the runway the engine blast took off the corrugated metal roof of a nearby shed sending the lethal sheets everywhere. Palm trees were bent to the ground, gravel was flying, and the refugee tents along with the refugees themselves sent hurtling through the air.

A few days later we landed at the same airstrip and as the ramp was full of airplanes we taxied onto the grass between the runway and ramp to park. After waiting a while for a spot to open up the IL-76 cranked engines and began taxiing for the runway, in a hurry and as bullheaded as ever. All of a sudden, I saw the British mechanic with us run out in front of the Russian airplane and made them stop. The left-wing tip of the IL-76 was 10 feet from ripping the tail and rudder off our beloved Herc. The flight crew started two engines and taxied the Herc farther out in the grass as the impatient IL-76 roared off. The British mechanic was hailed as a hero for days to come.   You can sure learn some of life's lessons in strange places and from unthought-of people.

One instance with an African native while on one of our food haul has had one of the most profound effects on the way I've looked at life since.

Up to that incident it was the same as any other trip. We landed, taxied in, got the Congo line going and offloaded the rice, beans, and wheat we had onboard. I had finished rolling up tie down straps and was standing around in the cargo-compartment of the airplane listening to the flight crew and some Red Cross workers talking. I'd just shuffled one foot when I felt a tug on my pant leg. Looking down I saw a native on his hands and knees indicating he wanted me to move my right foot. I did, and he then picked up two grains of spilled rice I had set my foot on. He put the rice in a plastic grocery bag and moved on searching for more. Where he had the luxury of finding a grocery bag in that jungle I'll never know.

I knew what he found was going to be his supper that night and you would have to be an oil company executive for that not to tug at your heart. I realized at that time I had no problems in life. To this day when I wonder how I'll make the monthly payments or look longingly at a new snow machine I know I can't afford, I remember that day in a far-off county where they have real problems.

This is one reason that I feel, and because there is currently no military draft, that all young adults out of high school should have to serve six months or so in the Peach Corp or a similar organization. They would see how a lot of the world lives and just maybe learn to appreciate how lucky most of us are to live under the conditions we have here in the USA.

Mentioning all the interesting and unworthy people I've met would be impossible, but I tried to narrate the ones you would find worthwhile reading.

Unimproved Strips...You Bet

CHAPTER 5 - CONDITIONS

Weather, while being the first topic of idle conversation, was also the first consideration affecting the job we did. It affected where we went, why we were there, and how long it took to accomplish the job at hand. It didn't matter if it was cold enough to freeze the swinging parts of a brass monkey, or hot enough to melt said monkey, the job had to be done.

"El Nino" in 1997 was a prime example of where we were called upon because of weather conditions. Papua, New Guinea, one of the wettest spots on earth, was experiencing a drought. Forest fires were rampant, and the river used to barge supplies up to the mine was all but dried up.

Barely home a week after nine weeks in PNG, I was sent to Peru to haul diesel fuel to a mine located in the Andes Mountains. One of the driest parts of the globe, the west coast of South American receives as much rainfall as politicians do common sense. Some people in Chili I talked to hadn't seen or felt rain fall in their lifetime. Now we were there because all of the roads were washed out and to keep the mine in operation, fuel needed to be airlifted.

Alaska's North Slope had the most severe weather conditions, other than Antarctica, you could possibly work in. Eskimos enjoyed living on their land, I liked just visiting. Trouble was, just like a mother-in-law visitation, I had way too many visits and some of too long a duration.

It was the wind I mostly hated, along with the blinding, stinging snow it carried. It hurt so bad at times you thought you were on a bird hunt with Dick Cheney. The Herc always had to be parked facing into the wind to prevent the frigid air from blowing in the exhaust holes and onto the hot turbines of the engines. This meant as you were pulling the load out of the back you had to look straight into the blowing snow to make sure the load cleared and didn't damage the airplane. Aluminum airplanes always lost the battle when put up against drilling steel.

Of course, you only had the chance for this pleasure if you found the mostly white runway in an all-white whiteout at a 150 mph. I can't stress enough the quality of the pilots it took to operate under the hazardous Arctic conditions.

Take, for example, the night we flew into..., well I don't remember the name of the lake or the village it was next to, but I do remember the landing.

They knew we were coming in, so when we did a low pass over the village, a fur clad Eskimo was sent out on a snow machine to light the antique flare pots placed on top of empty 55-gallon fuel drums. Our first approach showed only two pots lit so we went around. The second approach showed four pots lit with one flickering out as we roared overhead. The wind was blowing so hard the flare pots wouldn't stay lit as the Eskimo drove back and forth from pot to pot.

Our third approach was more successful with five pots lit, two on one side of the ice runway and three on the other side. It was enough to show us the direction of the runway, so we touched down, the airplanes landing lights faintly showed the sparse, lightless drums on each side of the nearly mile long runway. Ta, da, we're here.

This was just another trip in the log book for veteran pilot Dale Ranstead. It was just another change of underwear day for me.

Barter Island, located in the northeast corner of Alaska adjacent to the Eskimo village of Kaktovik, was one of the original DEW line sites. DEW (distant early warning) sites were radar stations during the Cold War with Russia. As such it had actual, genuine, electric runway lights you could sometimes see through the blowing snow. How we landed I don't know, but we were there so we figured we might as well offload. Only problem was the loader operator could not see well enough to find the airplane. It was necessary for me to walk out, find the loader, and lead him to the back of the Herc. I say "walk" if you can call leaning so far forward you could use your fingernails for 4-wheel drive assist, walking. This went on for each of the six pieces of freight we had on board.

To top things off as we were cranking engine number 3, the engine starter failed. Now it was the mechanics turn to earn that paycheck. And earn it he did, for it was often necessary to work barehanded to hook up connections to the motor. They earned my respect every time they put us back in the air and out of that weather.

Heading out west, not where the buffalo roam, but where the musk ox roam, is the coastal town of Pt. Lay. I've never checked in an encyclopedia on the subject of wind, but it is my belief that either the Aleutian Chain or PT. Lay is where it was invented. The wind is very proficient in both places. I've been to the Aleutians a few times and was privileged to see the log chain hanging from a pole that famed pilot Bob Reeves put up as a wind sock many years ago.

Back to Pt. Lay and yes, it's still windy, in fact that day it was extremely windy. The Herc was rocking back and forth in the blustery winds gusting over 45 knots. I don't remember why, but there were two loadmasters on board that day. That was a good idea for a lot of trips, but seldom happened. My longtime friend and one of my loadmaster trainers, Steve Scott was assigned the airplane and I was the helper.

The first piece of cargo was out the door with Steve giving the operator directions while I was inside the Herc preparing the rest of the cargo for offloading. As Steve was responsible for the aircraft I figured he should be outside to prevent the loader from damaging the airplane. The freezing cold 45 knot wind had nothing to do with my figuring.

As I finished removing a chain I looked out to see how things were progressing. The look was just in time to see a gust of wind take his feet right out from under him on that wind polished ramp. He landed flat on his back and was "gone with the wind" in an instant. The vision I had just witnessed out the airplane door put me in stitches.

I was rolling on the floor with tears freezing on my cheeks and I couldn't get up. The "instant replay" kept running through my semi-vacant head. Not very caring

I know, but what's a guy to do. I don't know how long it was before I saw Steve in a full 4-wheel drive, crawl to the loader, grab the rack, and stand up. The look on his face told me that he didn't find the incident nearly as amusing as I had. Well, hell, you're supposed to have some fun on the job, right?

Enough of the wind, after all it blows all over the world. Except on the North Slope, there it sucks.

How about just cold? If cold is what you're looking for, I know where to find it. I lived in the Yukon River Valley for 10 years. It holds the record low of -83° F recorded at Prospect Creek. I've never been out in -80 F temperatures. I know, I'm a wuss! I've only been out offloading fuel at -73° F. This was at an exploratory drill rig on the Awuna River west of Umiat. Added to that was a 20-mph wind putting the wind chill, I'm guessing, at -150°. I haven't seen a wind chill chart that covered those conditions.

The rubber fuel hose turned into steel pipe, and you couldn't be outside for more than five minutes at a time. Even with a facemask it was near impossible to breath the air, and from what I hear, air is pretty high on the necessity list. After we pumped the fuel off, the truck started to pull away. It was doing a good job of it too, until the transmission blew up and fluid and pieces fell to the ground. Luckily it had moved far enough to allow our wingtip to clear, so we could get the hell away from that lovely resort.

Back when Umiat had a weather station, 80% of the time, on the local TV weather report, it was the coldest spot in Alaska. Umiat, located on the Colville River at the edge of the northern foothills of the beautiful Brooks Range was a major hub for supplies, fuel, and base camp for much of the oil exploration of the North Slope. As such we flew in there many, many times. Every time we arrived the -55°F would greet our opening door and some of these trips were in July! I could have been off on my calendar a little though. I just recently learned the numbers and letters give you the information, not the bikini girls.

One humorous, though possibly devastating incident happened to us on the Umiat runway. We lined up for approach in the old tanked up Electra, threw out the rubber, and roared in to land. As we touched down a flock of hundreds of invisible white ptarmigan flew up hitting the nose cone and zooming past the cockpit toward the engines. We were sure the engines would suck 'em up and take out the turbines leaving us stranded. This never happened as the props were reversed just in time and ptarmigan went hurtling back past the cockpit. Some so close I could have reached out and grabbed them. You could tell by the expression on their face that they weren't used to flying backwards.

While we're on the North Slope let's think about anywhere else we would rather be. A favorite pastime, especially when Mother Nature called, facilities at a remote drill runway being what they were and all, as in non-existent, your local highest snow drifts having to suffice. When you gotta go, you gotta go, but it was as close to torture as I want to come. I know it's one of those seven deadly sins, but I envied the caribou, fox, and rabbits their furry ass!

On the Herc itself it was a different story, no facilities were available there either, but it was warmer and no wind. A solution was invented for those times you weren't going to make it to the next landing site. The solution was to carry as standard gear in your flight bag a supply of gallon size zip-lock baggies. They worked fairly well and were deposited at the next available receptacle.

Now I've never looked up Webster's definition of gymnastics but trying to crap in a plastic bag while flying through air turbulence has to come pretty close.

Getting rid of the enormous amounts of coffee we drank didn't give us quite as much exhilaration, but it had its moments. I mean at sixty below zero finding and getting out an inch and a half through 3 inches of clothing was a daunting task. And, if I remember right, it was at precisely -68.7° F you had to start backing up while urinating to prevent dire consequences. The North Slope is the only place I've been where you could get a frozen sperm sample without it having been ejected.

It was May and a balmy spring day, in Fairbanks anyway, Atqusak, a village 50 miles south of Barrow and our destination, was a different story entirely.

We loaded up in Fairbanks and as I grabbed my bag of winter gear for the trip I decided my bunny boots weren't needed. They were a pain to tie on the outside of my survival bag and I thought my leather boots would be enough. Sometimes I don't think so good.

Still winter in the Arctic, it was a not so balmy -45° at Atqusak when we landed. Out of my seat and into my Carharts, I was in the cargo compartment undoing chains as we taxied to parking. Soon after we parked the lights went out and I heard the GTC (ground turbine compressor) winding down, not a good sign.

The flight engineer had turned off the fuel switches to the four engines as he should have, but the fifth switch for the GTC should not have been touched. It was, and we were in big trouble. The fuel lines instantly went dry and could not be re-supplied with fuel. No fuel, no power, no lights, and no way to restart engines.

After finding out there would be no power it was flashlight time and hand pumping the backup hydraulic pump to open the door and let down the ramp. The cat operator backed the sled up to the Herc and we winched the load off of the airplane and onto the sled. While we were busy with the load the flight crew were devising a plan to get the engines running. After pumping the ramp and door shut I went up to the cockpit to see if I could help.

It was decided to take off the outside panel above the GTC, disconnect the fuel line and pour fuel down it. A jug and funnel were found, and fuel was drained from the wing tank. As the engineer and I poured fuel, the captain went in and lit off the GTC. It started up and ran but would only run up to 60% rpm. We tried again and again but couldn't gain anymore.

As you might imagine the wind and -45° temperature wasn't helping any. The cockpit had long since lost its heat and the only heat source was the cab of the cat, which was waiting the outcome of our endeavor. The crew tried to start an engine on the 60% GTC, but the engine would only spin up to about 40% rpm which was not enough to light it off. We were dead in the water, well dead on the ice was more appropriate.

We had been out in the cold for about an hour and by this time everyone was frozen. My survival bag had been emptied by yet another flight crew who didn't have sense enough to carry some arctic gear of their own. While most of my body was in fair condition, my feet in leather boots had long been frozen as I had been outside the longest.

There was nothing left to do but ride the cat the three miles to the village. As our limousine only had room for two people at a time in the cab with the Eskimo operator, we took turns every 10 minutes or so. Ten minutes in the luxury of a heated cab and ten minutes in coach class, until we reached town 45 minutes later.

That was the coldest I remember ever getting on this job, the agony of thawing my feet out has not been forgotten. On the bright side we were able to watch on satellite TV the first space shuttle take-off live. Also, it was a good chance to see government at work, for each state funded house had a fireplace in it...there wasn't a stick of wood for 300 miles in any direction!

Of course, all of the other loadmasters had stories to tell and this is one I found interesting.

Jim was on a fuel haul to a drill rig site on the North Slope. The offloading started off fine but, halfway through, the pump turned into a ball of ice and quit running. This was a common occurrence in the frigid – 60° F temperatures we encountered. The solution was to haul an empty 55-gallon drum in front of the GTC exhaust, have a ground crew member help you set the pump on it, and wait for it to thaw. This was done, and Jim was in the cargo compartment trying to thaw out himself with what little heat that's left there, at least he was out of the wind.

It was at this time the co-pilot came back wearing just a T-shirt expecting a short trip from the toasty warm cockpit. When he asked in a demanding voice what the hell was taking so long, Jim grabbed him by the knap of the neck and led him down the ramp and alongside the Herc to where the pump was thawing out. All the time with a tight hold on the co-pilots neck he explained slowly how this operation worked. Within seconds the co-pilots teeth were chattering, and he realized he had overstepped his bounds.

Jim kept on with his long explanation until finally, he asked the co-pilot if he would like to go back to his nice warm cockpit and mind his own business. I believe the co-pilot by this time was in full agreement. People skills were a big part of our job.

I'm chilly just writing about those times, let's take off our blankie and head to Africa.

While flying we had air conditioning in the Herc, but when we landed in the Congo jungle and opened the back door, the wall of heat would hit you with the same ferocity the North Slope cold did. The same GTC exhaust that would thaw a ball of ice at -60 below, could not even be felt when you walked through it. It was that hot!

Fortunately, the loads there were not labor intensive for me. Most of the loads were piece by piece and were loaded and unloaded by African labor. I only had to take care of the tie down and undoing cargo straps.

One condition that was hard to get used to in Africa was the things the natives carried with them. The women could carry a stack of sticks or a vase of water on the top of their head that would make me stagger, all the while carrying on a conversation with the kids or their friends.

The men and boys all carried an object that went with them where ever they went. Whether dressed in khakis or loin cloths, they all had one and were just looking for a chance to use it. It was a very useful tool they called AK-47s. They were used to coax the pilot to the head tent with all of our passports and they were also a handy item for obtaining a new camera, watch, shoes, and my new Leatherman. They had much more purchasing power than an American Express card.

I'm pretty sure none of them had been to a gun safety course because the guns were mostly pointed in the wrong direction namely mine. The main objective of this was to make sure the load got off in a hurry and we got the hell out of there. It sure worked, for that was my sentiment exactly.

After offloading one day I headed up front to the cockpit for one reason or another. I arrived just in time for a soldier coming through the crew door with his AK–47, while the captain at the top of the cockpit stairs was yelling "No guns allowed on my airplane!" I did the best "about face" I've done since boot camp and found something of more interest to do in the back of the airplane, like check my underwear.

Though we were "detained" at times we were never captured or held hostage, something that has happened. One Herc at one time hit a land mine on an airstrip and another came back with a bullet hole in the cockpit. To my knowledge we were never shot at, but who knows.

Some trips I missed out on in Africa were the airdrops. Food and supplies were dropped while flying overhead where there were no runways, or it was too dangerous to land. This generally happened in desert areas. I wish I could have done some of these.

I have seen photographs of a popular pastime loadmasters did after the cargo was dropped. This was to lengthen the line attached to their safety harness, put a small chain to hang on to through a couple of tie down rings on the ramp and wind surf out the back of the airplane. One loadmaster after doing his "thing" crawled back in the Herc, yanked on his tether line and pulled the tied down ring he had chosen out of the floor.

By the way it was a SAT loadmaster who rode out the door on a freight pallet in the movie "Air America."

Dealing with the customers who chartered the Herc contributed to the conditions a loadmaster worked under. Most were good to work for and relations were very good as long as we supplied their needs without much delay and didn't damage the goods. Some were a little more nit-picking than need be, but what was worse were ones who didn't supply much information at all. All of the priorities and figuring was left to us. There was one customer however who was inept, unprepared, and lacking any common sense, but they paid the best as money was no object, they wasted it like the town drunk.

Our government and its armed forces were the biggest pain in the ass we had the misfortune to deal with. We did a lot of flying for them because it was cheaper to pay us exorbitant rates than fly their own airplanes. You figure that out, I can't.

The waiting was probably the worst, how they supply a war I don't know. They demanded we be on time at the designated hour, and then we could wait for hours for the load to show up. When it did we would start the loading process only to have their equipment break down, causing more waiting time while it was replaced. You could also count on the same reception at the destination.

There was always someone there to impress you with his use of acronyms, which meant nothing to me. Obviously, it was a way to impress each other and lead to promotion to head idiot.

I think it was an airbase in Tennessee somewhere that we stopped for a load. As soon as I opened the cargo door a soldier ran up and asked me "what's your ACL?" With my natural blank look, I said "I don't know, what's an ACL?" "Available Cargo Load" was the reply. I told him to talk to the captain as I didn't know what the fuel weight would be. I'm sure "enough fuel to reach destination" wasn't on his acronym list.

The following story is an example of a normal military trip. The Air Force base we landed at was north of Salt Lake City, Utah with a destination close to home, Eielson Air Force Base 30 miles south of Fairbanks. The load was a typical military load; most of it on aluminum sheets covered with nets, the exception being a trailer mounted generator. Four sheets were pushed in on the afore mentioned Herc rollers, then came the generator which was pushed into position on the Herc. That left three aluminum pallets, two for the floor and one for the ramp.

The two pallets were pushed in and the last one overhung the ramp by a foot. The load length had been miscalculated which would interfere with shutting the ramp. "Oh, no" said one of the soldiers, "We'll have to unload and reload." I told them not to worry and bring the pallet for the ramp. With doubtful looks it was pushed in and I tied it down as far back as I could.

"How are you going to shut the ramp?" was their question. "Just watch." So, they all climbed in the airplane to watch. As the ramp came up the overhanging pallet rode up the ramp rollers and when the ramp and door were shut I tied the pallet down in place.

As the young soldiers cheered because they didn't have to off load and reload, one said "We could never do that on our Hercs." I know they couldn't, it's called improvising and isn't in the operations manual.

With a fueling stop in Billings, Montana, we headed north for Eielson. We landed and taxied in to our parking spot to offload. At Eielson the handling was done by Civil Service workers corrupted by military leaders.

The three pallets in the back were pushed onto a k-loader without a hitch. Next came the 2-ton generators and the problems began. Assuming we would take it off the same way it was put on I asked for the other K-loader in waiting to back up and we would push the generator on it.

"We can't do that" was the reply. "That's how we put it on" I said. "Don't matter, we can't do that here." We then pushed the generator back on the level ramp. "OK, have the fork lift pick it off." Can't do that either" the lead man replied. So, I then chained the generator to a ramp ring and lowered it to the ground. Next, I applied the generator parking brake and put the portable ramps we carry with us for rolling stock on the end of the ramp.

"Have the forklift come up behind the generator and we'll ease it off on the ground." "Can't do that" was the broken record reply. "Well how do you suggest we get it off?" was my by now impatient question. "I don't know" was the helpful answer.

By now I'd had it with the proceedings, so I popped the chain holding the generator and all of a sudden it was unloaded. I had expected the parking brake to partially slow the generator, but it worked as well as the rest of their equipment and the generator rolled 50 feet across the asphalt.

Now the lead man came alive with ideas, like what was my name and what was our contract number. I told him I could get the first question right but had no idea on the second.

While they could sit around all day and accomplish very little, something they were very good at, we were a revenue-based air carrier and we needed to move on to the next customer. Airplanes stalled on the ground were about as profitable as selling D-cup bras in China.

Another branch of government we dealt with on a regular basis was the FAA. Overseeing aviation in the USA being their primary responsibility, it is a necessary but incompetent government organization. They are basically paper chasers with a habit of coming up with the dumbest rules imaginable, all the while completely missing the issues that really need attention.

For years I had escaped any major confrontation with them and always hoped my good luck would continue. It was not to be, and I blame myself for not seeing this episode coming.

Willow Run Airport in Ypsilanti, Michigan was home base for our Herc when we were hauling auto parts. That day we had put on our load of auto parts and had taken off for our assembly plant destination. Shortly after takeoff we had to shut down an engine with gear box problems. We radioed the tower with our problem and turned and returned to the airfield. We parked right in front of the FAA building so as not to block a cargo loading zone.

After shutting engines down and opening the crew door a FAA representative came on board to check things out. After climbing up to the cockpit and finding out it was a normal engine shutdown he came back to the cargo compartment where I was. That was when I should have noticed that look in his eye, that look that said, "I need to show a reason for my paycheck!"

He looked around for a while and finally pointed to the electric pallet jack we used for moving cargo around and asked if that was the way it was when we took off. Knowing there was nothing wrong with the way the jack and cargo were tied down I said "yes."

"You don't have any strap keeping the pallet jack from moving a foot." he informed me. There were two straps lying on the floor I had undone to make it easier walking through the cargo compartment. If I had it to do over again, I would have told him that one of them was over the jack. I didn't think of it then and anyway it would have been a lie.

The pallet of cargo still on the jack was double tied down, this along with the brake set on the jack itself and fully chained down cargo a foot behind the jack meant that it wasn't going anywhere.

"I'm going to have to write you up for insufficient tie down" announced the FAA agent. I couldn't believe my ears. It was as plain as day it couldn't move.

This "write up" when sent to the company was accompanied with a hefty fine amounting to thousands of dollars. When questioned by the cargo supervisor, I told him what had happened and how the load was tied down. LAC (Lynden Air Cargo) backed me up and decided to fight the accusation. Paperwork flew back and forth for months and finally a test of my tie down ability was devised.

A pallet of cargo and jack were tied down like I had it in the airplane. Next a strap was run from the jack to a forklift outside the airplane with a scale in between to measure the amount of "G" force required to move the jack. The jack weighed 1,000 pounds which meant it had to survive 2,000 pounds of pull pressure to meet the 2

G's required for aft restraint. The loader pulled to twice that and more.

I wasn't there for the test in Anchorage but received a copy of the letter written by the Chief of Operations to the FAA exonerating me from all guilt. The matter was dropped, but I wonder what the cost was to taxpayers and my company to comply with an inept FAA agent.

A few years ago, a heavily criticized "do nothing" FAA grounded all MD-80's at the same time for a "possible" wheel well electrical fire. This put air travel in turmoil for weeks and was a good example of government organizations incompetence. A good airplane mechanic would vouch for what I believe was something that could have been done at each individual airplanes next major check.

The FAA tries to do something that makes them look good instead of working on things that need attention. Our antiquated and very dangerous Air Traffic Control system is a good example. If the TCAS (traffic collision alert system) screen that is in the cockpit of all airlines was transmitted to that little TV screen in the seat back in front of you, many of you would be walking.

The experiences that have happened to me while flying and in my private life, along with newscasts concerning government agencies, has led me to believe that they're all incompetent or crooked, or both. Show me one agency, FAA, BLM, FEMA, FDA, IRS, FBI, CIA, etc., that lives up to the qualifications of your average every day kindergarten class and I'll eat my hat. If you know of one...please contact me at my remote Alaskan homestead at BR-549.

While I was in Croatia in 1995, an incident that happened in Croatia shows that the USA doesn't corner the market on government deception. We were based in Zagreb, Croatia with three Hercs flying supplies for our Armed Forces into Bosnia.

One day, as I headed to the coffee shop in the elaborate, marble adorned lobby of the Zagreb Intercontinental Hotel, I had a chance to overhear a conversation not meant for my ears I'm sure. A NATO general was talking to some soldiers in the center of the lobby. As I passed them I heard the command "Now get out there in your vehicles and make it look like we're doing something! "As the cat on the couch next to me is my witness, this was an actual command from a NATO general during a time of war! Looking out of my hotel room window you could see NATO pickups running all over the place, just a driver and no cargo. They must have fooled somebody.

"Time is of the essence," "Time is money", "time stands still," time is many things, but it is one thing that is constant. Only the way you look at it changes. Twenty minutes at the dentist's office or twenty minutes of sex, were they the same amount of time?

Time is also how a record is set, either the fastest, or the longest. Time for most of us determines how much we are paid in wages and unfortunately, time measures how little sleep we sometimes get.

Same as truck drivers pile up hours upon hours on the road, so do flight crews pile up hours in the air. While it is the number of miles driven that distinguishes truck drivers, it is still the thousands of hours of flying time that distinguishes pilots. Loadmasters are like Rodney Dangerfield, we get no respect!

There were times we felt like just another piece of the airplane. The flight crew you were flying with would get off and a new crew would get on and off we'd go. Loadmasters had no time restrictions for flying. Sometimes we were on the airplane for 3 or 4 days with only a break to borrow someone's hotel room shower. Sandwiches became known as "fine cuisine" and naps on the Herc's bunk almost made you feel like you had some sleep. I always said "just because I'm lying on the bunk doesn't mean I'm sleeping", just like "just because I'm standing up doesn't mean I'm awake".

My first year on the Electra I was paid by the amount of block time accumulated, same as the flight crew. Block time being wheel chock to wheel chock, basically the time the airplane is moving. An average month was around 180 hours with 232 hours being the highest, about twice as much time as pilots were allowed to fly in a month. Most pilots with most airlines can fly 100 hours a month and 1,000 hours in a year. This is controlled by the FAA in a very complicated set of rules, of course.

This time keeping method gives a false idea of the real time involved. With a loadmaster you can add in the loading and offloading time. With flight crews you have to figure in showing up early for paperwork, checking the weather and checking out the aircraft, then staying late for more paperwork. For all of us were the travel time, weather hold, and occasional maintenance problems.

This leads up to people with a lot of responsibility putting in very long days. That is why we hear so much on the news these days about pilot fatigue. It's a true story.

The highest concentrated hours, that I can remember, was a hitch on the Herc. We flew a commercial airline from Anchorage to Edmonton, Canada to pick up the Herc from a "C-check." A "C-check" is a major going over of the airplane required after so many hours of flight time. We took the airplane and headed to Florida to do some runs to Honduras, after which we went back to Ypsilanti, Michigan to haul auto parts. Two weeks later with 2 or 3 flight crews and just little old me taking care of the cargo, I thought it was time to do a little checking. I thought it was time to do a little complaining too, but who the hell listens to a loadmaster, especially a whiny one?

I opened the log book knowing it was zeroed out at the c-check and found I'd logged 160.4 hours of flight time in 14 days. This marathon ended a couple of days later when an injury landed me in the Ypsilanti emergency room. I fell asleep on the table while they were checking my injury out. That two week pay period my time sheet tallied 240.5 hours.

I've logged a lot of hours of flight time, but there are many people in aviation with a lot more than me. I have seen in aviation magazines where retiring pilots have accrued 35,000 hours of flight time. There would be very few with much more than that. Those logged hours are deceptive as to the amount of "real flying" hours. Take a major air carrier captain for example. After attaining some seniority, he can bid a line where he flies non-stop from Dallas, Texas to London, England and back the next day. He has accumulated a lot of time, but 90% of that was on auto-pilot. He does a few of these trips and he is out of flying time for the month.

Now take my friend and lifelong pilot Holger "Jorgy" Jorgensen as an example of a real pilot. In his recent published book "Jorgy," he states that he logged 34,500 hours of flight time. Most of this time was "bush flying" in Alaska, with some in Africa and various parts of the world. Though having a lot of time carrying passengers, most of his time was cargo hauling. This type of flying here in Alaska required landing and taking off from river bars, ocean shore, ice strips, grass or gravel strips, and sometimes even the tundra itself. In all this time he only slightly damaged one airplane.

Out of the hundreds of pilots I've flown with I believe because of the concentrated flying of those years, the few pilots, and even fewer loadmasters, I have more flying time with Jorgy than any other pilot. I've always considered myself very fortunate and privileged to spend that time with such a great man.

A while ago a current Herc captain who used to fly co-pilot with Jorgy invited him on a Herc ride for old time sake. I was working for the ground handler at the time and worked overtime to get the loads built ahead so I could go along on that "historic" occasion. After takeoff, Jorgy was invited to sit in the co-pilot's seat. Being mostly blind now he was unable to fly the airplane, I still would rather fly with him blind than some of the pilots I have flown with. I noticed after he sat down he reached around and moved the seat controls to suit him, like it was yesterday he sat in that seat, instead of the 32 years it had been since he was on a Herc. He always knew every part of every airplane he ever flew.

On the return trip we talked over old times and places. Jorgy mentioned that one day on the Herc he and loadmaster Terry Paz had done 13 round trips from one oil drill site to another. Sometimes it was just a 10-minute hop for a rig move on the slope. Nowadays a huge tire equipped flatbed truck called a Roll-a-gone would do the job, back then it was the Herc to the rescue.

I remember one day we had done 13 round trips out of Camp Lonely. This is about as many trips a shift I have heard of. It was such a short trip the landing gear was left down, and I could barely do the paperwork. That night was spent eating supper through closed eyes and dragged my feet to bed. I'd handled more chains that day than Laurence Welk did bubbles.

For those of you who like to Funk with your Wagnalls, that was 52 take-offs and landings mostly on ice strips in one day. More than most pilots log in a month.

Lockheed Martin acknowledges flight crew members with over 20,000 hours in one of their C-130 Hercules and the Air Force gave out pins for loadmasters with 10,000 hours. Very few people have attained these awards.

I have to give recognition to a loadmaster who started a few years before me, helped teach me my job, and continued to fly up to a couple years ago. He was one of the best and is considered a legend in his field today. I believe he has more flying hours than anybody in the world, alive or dead. Steve Scott has done it all and done it well!

Our flight time was only part of it, usually the first one to the airplane and the last one to leave it, we easily piled up the most time in, on, and around the Herc. I've always had, and I always will have a special place in my heart for the Herc, but there were times I just wanted off.

Cus-Cus, Papua, New Guinea

Jorgy The Chief!

CHAPTER 6 - ADVENTURE

While I'm not one of those people with a thirst for adventure, a little doesn't hurt, it alleviates boredom. I couldn't stand a "stuck in the office" type of job, but neither would I apply for the position of daredevil, mountain climber, bull rider or parachute jumper. The job of loadmaster fits nicely somewhere in between. There were times the paperwork had me feeling like an office worker, but there were also times we were attempting mountain climbing, only we would have been starting and staying at the top.

Flying over Mt. McKinley looking down was my way of viewing the top of North America. It looked like a nice place that I wouldn't want to visit. We've seen the climbers and their small tents, and I much preferred our cozy warm cockpit, as long as the engines stayed running.

As flying hours and experience piled up it took a little more danger to threaten my underwear. On my maiden voyage as a loadmaster we had barely cleared the end of the runway when a recorded voice blared out "Pull up, pull up." We were going up, what the hell did he want? Maybe we weren't going up enough and were going to crash were my instant thoughts. A malfunctioning altitude alert system was to blame, we were doing just fine, after my heart slowed down to a machine gun rate that is. I would have liked to put a DMI sticker over that guy's mouth, him and his buddy who always liked to exclaim "Terrain, Terrain" when we were in the middle of a cloud.

The Lockheed Electra was the first airplane I spent a lot of time in and the first to start my transition from dark hair to white. One of the first mishaps I remember came one night we were on a Styrofoam run. Well mostly Styrofoam, we had four pallets of dynamite on board as well.

Everything was fine until we were ready to land on the lake ice at Ivotuk. The landing gear was lowered but we couldn't get an indication light for the nose gear. We flew around several times recycling the landing gear, no light. The gear was put back up and we headed back to Fairbanks to deal with the problem there.

Fairbanks was notified by radio we were declaring an emergency and plans were being made there and in the cockpit. Jorgy was at the controls and devised our plan of action. He decided we would buzz the tower to get a visual on the nose gear then come around for an approach. We would land normal, setting the main gear on then easing the nose wheels down. If the nose gear collapsed Jorgy would call for flaps back to 50% and max power to take off and go around for another attempt knowing we would crash this time.

What impressed me the most was that he asked each one of us if that plan was O.K. Even me, what the hell did I know? The co-pilot, engineer, and me all agreed with the plan. All I knew was a crash and burn with thousands of pounds of dynamite on board would make for some spectacular fireworks.

Obviously, the Fairbanks Airport Fire and Rescue team thought the same way, for as we approached the airfield we could see the runway was lined with fire trucks and emergency vehicles of all kinds. Red lights were flashing everywhere waiting for our arrival. That's when the reality of it all set in, their waiting on us. Us! Not until the flashing lights were visible did I get nervous.

We made a pass in front of the tower and were informed the nose gear was down, but there was no way to tell if it was locked in place. We went around and lined up on the runway for the landing. Jorgy greased it in on the main gear and began to ease the nose down. When the wheels touched he held it even for a ways, but we had to find out if the gear would hold while there was still enough runway left to take off again.

Putting more weight on the nose gear it felt like it was holding so we went ahead and stopped. The mechanic raced up in his truck and put a pin in the gear to make sure it would hold while we taxied to parking.

It turned out to be just an indication light fault. Unlike the "check engine" light in today's cars that come on when the license plate is dirty, you have to believe your lights and instruments in an airplane. That time the lights lied to us, the next instance they most defiantly did not.

The trip to Ivotuk just north of the Brooks Range with a load of fuel was uneventful. The return trip was anything but.

We roared off the ice strip and headed home. As the bright moonlight illuminated the beautiful and rugged mountains of the Brooks Range ahead of us, we headed up a valley on our climb out. All of a sudden, all hell broke loose, air turbulence grabbed us and we were being pushed up so hard my chin went to my knees. Seconds later we were going down so hard the pilot couldn't pull his arm with the microphone down to his mouth. Then again back up, then down with terrible force. Luckily each time we went down it was between mountain peaks; then again back up, each time hoping this time would be the one to take us up and out of this horror.

This was not to be, down again we were slammed, down for so long and hard that the fuel went to the top of the tanks and oil went to the top of the engines. The low fuel and oil lights came on. Bells were ringing, buzzers were buzzing, lights were flashing, and pearly gates were opening. At the last instant we were again forced up, how long could the wings take this?

As quick as it started the turbulence ended as we were thrown up and out of it. How long did it last? Certainly more than a minute and slightly less than a decade. The cockpit was deathly quiet until the co-pilot who was flying at the time said something stupid like "Wasn't that something?" It did ease the tension somewhat. At least he could speak, I wasn't sure my teeth were still in my mouth.

We hadn't flown along very far when the crew began to realize, something wasn't right. A check on the Loran confirmed their suspicions. We were bucking an unforecasted 220-knot headwind and weren't making much headway.

At this time, we were nearing the small settlement of Bettles, a waypoint on the airways north of Fairbanks. Bettles didn't have much, a lodge, post office, store, and a few cabins, but it did have an airstrip long enough to land the Electra on and more important at this juncture, fuel. As the flight engineer started calculations on fuel consumption I looked down at the lights of Bettles. The gauges were read, and the calculator was pulled out, I looked down at the lights of Bettles. As figures were being figured and engine power settings contemplated, I looked down at the lights of Bettles. The calculations were near done, and a decision was close at hand, I looked down at the lights of Bettles. The engineer was finished with calculations and the decision was made to continue on to Fairbanks, we had enough fuel. I looked down at the friendly lights of Bettles.

There wasn't a hint of a place to put the Electra down between Bettles and Fairbanks, we were committed. No other problems surfaced on our way to Fairbanks and on decent everything looked fine. Fine, that is, until all four low fuel lights came on and stayed on! The lights of Fairbanks were well in sight, but for some reason they didn't seem to be getting any closer, least ways not fast enough for us.

After we used up what was left of that decade, we were lined up for the runway and there were those damned flashing red lights again. As we crossed the big white stripes on the end of the runway a sigh was felt rather than heard through the cockpit. Touchdown felt especially good and as we slowed to turn on the taxiway, two engines shut down due to lack of fuel. The other two engines propelled us to parking where they were shut down on purpose. We weren't flying anymore that night, this airplane needed an inspection.

When the airplane was inspected the G forces recorded went into the category of "extreme turbulence" and two wing cracks were found. It was a couple of hours and more than a few shots of whiskey, the first two poured down me by a friendly waitress, due to my inability to hold a glass. After that I decided a little episode like this wasn't going to end my career in aviation.

I'm not so sure that was a good decision, but the only other occupation I had was meat cutter and a taste of flying told me I couldn't be trapped in a butcher shop anymore. It would have been less dangerous and more profitable, but who wants to sweat like that?

Landing on ice runways is what we did. It was the only practical solution in the frozen Arctic. When the temperature was cold, as it usually was, the roughed-up ice allowed ample steering and braking action. When it warmed up above freezing it was a different matter.

Liberator Lake was another supply camp for the smaller seismic crew exploring for oil. The fuel we hauled in to their storage tanks was transferred to smaller airstrips, usually by a Twin Otter.

Back in the 70's, May 15th was considered the average cut-off date for using ice strips on the North Slope. Today it would be sometime in April. You have to consider that back then was before Al Gore's hot air started thawing the Arctic.

We were stretching the time frame that trip as it was the middle of May. On approach that warm, sunny day everything looked fine, so we touched down. Reversing props and applying brakes put things into action and none of them good. The airplane at times was almost sideways and the outboard props were in danger of hitting the snow banks on either side of the runway at any time. The pilot managed to straighten us out, but more than half of the runway was used up by now.

The pilot started shouting "I can't stop it!" the co-pilot was shouting "stop it, Stop it!" The flight engineer was shouting "Hold it, hold it!" and the loadmaster was shouting but nothing came out. At times like this you need something intelligent to say and that left me out. The hill at the end of the runway was fast approaching while the pilot fought to get us stopped. The less used end of the runway had better ice and we managed to stop just in time.

I won't say how close it was, but when we turned around the wingtip put a mark in the snow on the hillside.

We taxied back up the runway to the taxiway leading to the ramp. After parking I opened the side cargo door and put the aluminum ladder down to the ice. The bottom of the ladder was sitting in two inches of water.

The tail stand, SPR, and hoses were quickly hooked up and the pump turned on. I followed the crew up to the shack for some coffee and donuts, thinking whiskey would be better about now.

After a quick shot of coffee, I headed back to the Electra. As I neared the airplane I found myself walking in six inches of water. The ice was collapsing under the weight of the loaded airplane! Rushing up the ladder I turned the pump up to maximum and headed up to the shack to inform the crew.

When the offloading was completed, engines were being cranked while I stashed the equipment. I hated working around spinning props especially on ice but it was time to get a move on. We hastened to leave before the ice collapsed and were lucky enough to make it off.

This wouldn't have been the first airplane to go through the ice stretching the season in the quest for oil on the North Slope.

While water is sometimes the culprit in aviation, fire always is.

Fuel was barged into Camp Lonely's holding tanks during the summer and during winter we were often based there hauling fuel to drill sites. It was always colder than a tin outhouse and dodging rabid foxes was about the only excitement available.

Enter an engine fire stage left, actually stage right, as it was number four engine that burst into flames shortly after takeoff that day. Lonely's radio was notified we were coming back in with an engine fire as we turned back for the runway.

The fire extinguisher bottle was activated, and the fire flickered out only to reignite. The second bottle was discharged as we approached the runway, this one having much more effect. The engine was only smoking as we roared by the ramp on the runway and by the time we parked only needed a short burst from a fire extinguisher mounted on a handcart.

The two fire extinguisher carts pushed by men and a Suburban with one lonely beacon were a far cry from a

Fairbanks reception, but at the time we were very glad to see them.

Of course, all of our flights were not like these, most were just plain normal, and some were down right pleasurable. The sightseeing was an added bonus, especially when it was something rare we had a chance to see.

Ivotuk base camp was a popular destination on our fuel haul list and being in the north side foothills of the Brooks Range was very picturesque. Added to this for a few days was a huge herd of caribou. Fish and Game biologists studying the herd informed us that there were between eighty and one hundred thousand caribou. How they count them, I'm not sure, but I'd heard it was a simple matter of counting their legs and dividing by four.

We followed the herd for several days until they were out of justifiable fuel range. The herd would cover a whole mountain and more, it reminded me of bees covering a hive. Very few people have ever gotten the chance to see something like this and we considered ourselves very lucky.

Viewing wildlife was a popular pastime on this job whenever possible. Moose, caribou, bear, musk ox, Dall sheep, wolves, and arctic fox were able to be seen as we flew overhead. Some also caused close calls as we had to abort takeoffs and landings due to their presence on the runway.

One day as we were climbing out of Umiat, the flight engineer looked out the left side of the cockpit and spotted a grizzly bear taking down a caribou. The captain throttled back, and we circled to see this spectacle of nature. Looking for something specific from an airplane is very hard; just ask the Coast Guard, we never spotted the bear. Several circles were made with everyone looking to no avail, and then the co-pilot interrupted our concentration with some trivial thing about our airspeed being next to stall speed. The captain grabbed a handful of throttle and it was back to work.

Another memorable trip for me originated out of Umiat. We had climbed to 10,000 feet headed for Barrow when Jorgy called Anchorage Center requesting VFR clearance. It was granted and as he pulled back on the power levers Jorgy said, "Let's go wolf hunting." Down to the deck we went, cruising along to see what we could see. No wolves were spotted, or he would have "petted" them with the wing tip. All we saw was a white arctic fox running across the snow. To see that at well over 250 mph might give a hint as to how low we were.

N404 GN, one of GNA's Electra's had a quirk in it, one that had happened once before the night I was onboard. I don't know the particulars of that time, other than Jorgy was at the controls then as he was this night.

We were headed south to Fairbanks after dropping off a load of fuel somewhere on the Slope. About halfway back as I fought to keep my eyes open, all of a sudden there were two loud clicks, then total darkness. We had lost all electrical power, and I do mean all, no back up system, nothing. The engines kept running or I'd be having a hard time writing this now, forty years later.

The engineers did a thorough check, but nothing could be done to get power back. It was in the black of night and we were down to about as many instruments as Wilbur and Orville had. The weather was clear and soon the glow of the lights of Fairbanks were visible. No problem finding the airport, but what to do when we arrived there.

Without electrical power we had no landing gear indication, no landing lights, no instruments or cockpit lights, and no fasten seatbelt sign. With the radio working off the battery Fairbanks airport of course knew we were coming. We did what seemed by now the "standard operating procedure" of buzzing the tower and lining up on all the flashing red lights. The landing went without a hitch and soon I was doing my "standard operating procedure," downing a few shots of whiskey.

As far as I know what caused that glitch was never found and it never happened again.

My logbook of Electra times wouldn't be complete without a crash. No disappointment there.

There always has to be your first time, on this particular night it was the pilot's first flight after being checked out as captain. I'm sure that just like a first solo flight for a pilot's license, your first flight as a Captain is a nervous time. Now, you are the man, and no one is there to bail you out.

We loaded up and took off with the fuel load destined for the remote drill site, Ikipikpuk, somewhere south of Barrow. The weather was good, some wind, but no blowing snow and the ice strip with its two rows of runway lights was easily visible. The weather shack was notified we were there and the approach was set up.

As we descended to the runway, gear down, flaps full, the co-pilot was calling out our airspeed. Closing in on the landing the airspeeds were all wrong, much too slow and we all knew it. We waited for the boost of power that was needed from the pilot, but it never came. Gravity came, and we fell out of the air a full sixty feet and slammed onto the ice. Why the plane never broke, I don't know, my back felt like it had.

We taxied to parking and pumped the fuel off; all the while I was deciding whether or not to get back on the airplane. Finally, not wanting to be stuck in a place called Ikipikpuk won out and I closed the door and flew back.

Making a mistake is one thing, not owning up to it is another. Upon our return the lowlife pilot, never called for an overweight or hard landing inspection and said nothing about what happened. The airplane went on flying for almost a week before the co-pilots conscience couldn't let this go on and an inspection was called for. Two wing cracks were found, grounding the airplane for a while. The pilot went on flying for the company and years later piled up a MarkAir jet.

After this instance I took to asking who was flying when the dispatcher called me to report to work. A while had passed when this pilots name was issued as the one I'd be flying with. I told the dispatcher I wouldn't fly with this man again, that he had had his only chance to kill me he was going to get. I was told I would fly or be fired, I chose the latter.

Two days later the phone rang and I was asked to come back to work. "I thought I was fired" was my reply. "We need you" he admitted. "Who's flying?" I asked. "Jorgy." "I'll be right out." I went on flying for many years after that with only a couple of times of serious thought of refusing.

There is one last Electra experience I would like to relate.

Many types of aircraft were called upon to fulfil the jobs required to find oil on the North Slope. From passenger jets to single engine airplanes and everything in between each had its function. Helicopters were very prolific on the slope due to the lack of runways and the specific jobs that only they could do.

The sun that barely peeks over the horizon in early spring on the North Slope had just went back into hiding as we approached the drill site of Tunalik. Located in the far northwestern part of the Slope it was one of our longest trips. As we approached the runway and its adjacent parking ramp the ground controller informed us that a helicopter was preparing to lift off from the ramp.

Just as the chopper came into sight it's crew informed us via radio that it was cranking the engine and would depart to the east in a couple of minutes. Our co-pilot acknowledged him and that we would swing to the west circle around and land. "O.K. thanks we'll catch you later" was their reply.

We flew on, throwing out the landing gear, downing the flaps and started our circle for approach to the runway. As we came around, there on the tundra a couple of hundred yards from the runway was the helicopter totally engulfed in flames. We were the last people they ever talked to.

This instance, along with a helicopter two years earlier that had crashed in my uncle's yard a few miles out of Fairbanks, burning four men to death in front of his family, has given me a deep mistrust of helicopters. With all the helicopter crashes since then and the rash of recent ones at this writing, both military and civilian, nothing has or will change my opinion.

A few years back a rookie co-pilot told a few of us that God had told him to get out of helicopters. I thought it was very rude of him for not finishing listening, for his obvious ineptness led me to believe he was told to get out of aviation altogether before he killed innocent people.

The Electra was a fine airplane and I had a lot of good times with a lot of good people while flying on them. In Jorgy's book I was mildly surprised to find out that of all the different airplanes he flew, that the Electra was his favorite. It would have been my favorite too, if it wasn't for the cramped, rock hard contraption called a jump seat I spent so many hours in. For that reason, the C-130 Hercules with a spacious cockpit and a couch for hard working loadmasters was my favorite.

The transition from the Electra to the Herc went fairly smooth with the experienced loadmasters showing me the ropes, chains would be more appropriate. One of the first things I noticed was the lack of DMI (deferred maintenance item) stickers plastered about the cockpit. A much better maintenance program meant less mechanical breakdowns, which in turn meant that underwear lasted longer these days.

The one thing that didn't change was the fact that all the flying was still on the North Slope. On the Electra fuel hauls, most of the trips were back and forth from Fairbanks, on the Herc we were based up north for a month or more at a time.

This meant a constant bout with the North Slope weather, which I was more than familiar with already.

The frequency and rapidity that a whiteout could move in was notorious, at times causing some anxious moments.

We could takeoff and enroute the destination would sock in, worse yet a check without departure point would show the weather was down there also. A radio check with all suitable runways within a reasonable distance, reasonable distance meaning enough fuel to get there, could be socked in. This left us flying around looking for a place to land; all the while the fuel gauges were getting ready to land on zero.

This happened more than once and was the reason you would hear the captain telling the engineer to put on a little extra fuel for the wife and kids. Finally, it was down to picking a runway and finding it no matter what. This was an experience guaranteed to keep everyone's heart rate up. While I can't remember ever getting down to fumes, there were some who had, making that landing attempt mandatory. A tough way to make a living in anybody's book.

The west coast of Alaska is one of the places I've always suspected bad weather was invented; at the very least it is well practiced there. That trip to the village of Wales was a perfect example.

As we approached the runway luck was with us, a temporary lull in the storm allowed the runway to be seen for a minute and Mike "Red Dog" Redman slipped us in. We slowly taxied to the ramp at the very end of the runway. A renewed effort by the storm made visibility about as clear as a politician's interview. Progress was made with each lull in the wind until we reached the parking spot.

The load was a couple of windmill generators and miscellaneous cargo. With so many pieces to handle and an equally complex back haul we were there for a long time. No matter, the storm was patiently waiting for us.

The engines were cranked, warmed up, flaps set for takeoff, and crew briefing done. We were ready to go, but where? We couldn't see a thing. Finally, a small break in the storm allowed us to taxi to the runway where it was immediately obscured. When the runway came back into view Red Dog turned onto it and we blasted down it. Part way down the runway and way before flying sped we lost everything. Aborting takeoff and staying on the runway wasn't likely. The hill to our right was invisible and could soon be the hill in front of us. Red Dog instantly made the only decision we had left, he pulled us into the air to hang on the props.

Hanging on the prop was usually a last resort effort done by single engine bush pilots on too short airstrips. Hanging on the prop was the process of lifting off and hoping the propeller forced enough air between the wing and ground to keep you airborne until flying speed was reached.

The Herc with its four powerful engines and large wings turned out to be good at this too. We roared out of there on a wing and I'm sure somebody said a prayer. While it worked this time I'm sure the whole crew would agree it would never be a standard operating procedure.

The powerful prop blast of the Herc was the source of entertainment several times. My entertainment, not the people on the receiving end.

Spring had invaded the North Slope and while delivering a heavy load of fuel we were met with a soft, muddy runway and ramp.

I was in the back of the Herc with the ramp and door open as we taxied in a big circle to park next to the fuel tanks. Suddenly the airplane tilted to the right as the right main gear found a deep mud hole in the gravel ramp. Not wanting to get stuck the captain added power, a lot of power to pull through to firm ground.

People dove for cover as the instant hurricane tore through the camp. Anything loose was gone, a stack of ¾" plywood looked like a deck of playing cards as it scattered across the tundra. The clincher was a man who opened the door to his ATCO unit room to see what was going on. The door was ripped from his grasp, tore off the hinges and sent out in the tundra. It lasted less than a minute until firm ground was attained and thankfully no one was injured.

Another time, damage could have been prevented and I tried, but some people have to learn the hard way.

People in remote villages would sometimes purchase a home building kit in Alaska's two major cities, Anchorage or Fairbanks and have it flown in, the cost of transportation included in the purchase price. Normally everything for a house, building material, windows, doors, roofing, appliances, and furniture would fit in one Herc load.

We were on such a trip to a small village in western Alaska. This trip was for an addition and upgrade to a hunting and fishing lodge. Everything you can imagine was onboard, including the proverbial kitchen sink.

The runway was short and the ramp small, but we managed to pull in and turn around facing the runway. As we started offloading I noticed they were putting everything on the far edge of the small ramp directly behind the Herc. Knowing what would happen when we applied power to taxi to the runway for departure, I suggested that they might want to stack the items off to one side. I was told it would be alright and we continued to offload. Everything was finally all off as people admired all the new lodge upgrades in pieces as they envisioned the completed project.

I raised the ramp up until just before it latched, leaving the upper door open. Informing the flight crew that the "door open light" would remain on and that I would shut the door when we reached the runway, the mechanic and I went back to watch the proceedings.

While engines were being cranked people ran for the safety of their vehicles. When power was applied to taxi away the fun began. Bundles of insulation were instantly sent into the trees, refrigerators and stoves were toppled over and slid across the gravel, and the last thing we saw as I closed the door, was the new blue couch, still in plastic wrap clearing the tops of the 40-foot trees. That must have been some scavenger hunt after we left.

Remote lodges were always calling on the Herc for equipment and building supplies. One in particular was a huge mansion on Lake Clark west of Anchorage, built by an Anchorage millionaire, at last count it was up to 23 Herc loads. Another lodge was one on Chandalar Lake up in the Brooks Range and it brought with it two memorable trips.

Chandalar Lake was a beautiful spot surrounded by snowcapped mountains, a veritable paradise anyone would love having a cabin on. These were my thoughts as we flew over the deep blue lake, that is until I spotted the tiny dirt runway we were to land on. The runway started right on the lakeshore, climbed a little hill before leveling off, and ended at the foot of a mountain which said loud and clear "No go around!"

With three pieces of heavy equipment on board we were heavy and as we approached, the runway looked smaller and smaller. The well qualified pilot hoping to use the entire short runway, touched down on the rising hill. We hit too hard and bounced back into the air, by the time we touched down again most of the runway was behind us. The pilot hit max reverse with the props and stood on the brakes. We stopped with a little runway left and a lot of held breath escaping our lungs. As we exited the airplane the next danger was a fire from the overheated brakes. We lucked out and there wasn't any, but they all had to be replaced back in town. In my recollections this was the biggest test of my tie down job ever and a perfect example of why a loadmaster had to do his job right.

The second trip to Chandalar Lake was in the winter time. The little dirt strip was unusable for the Herc at this time and a runway was plowed out on the lake ice. The load wasn't much as the main reason for the trip was to haul the heavy equipment back out.

The mountains were engulfed in a snowy white haze almost down to the lake, leaving us little visibility as we sneaked up the valley leading to the lake and its dead-end ring of mountains. We were told where the runway was on the lake, but with the whiteout conditions it was nearly impossible to find.

As we circled the lake looking for something that looked like a runway, Red Dog commented to the only other old timer in the crew, me, "Reminds ya of the old days, huh, Tup." Looking for an ice runway in a whiteout did remind me of the old days when he and I spent a lot of time scaring ourselves. What I didn't remember in the North Slope days was the disturbing fact that we were now flying around looking up at spruce trees.

We did find the runway before using the props as chainsaws and Paul Harvey has the rest of the story.

Speaking of spruce trees, we did hit the wingtip on one while landing at the narrow dirt airstrip at Venetie. This small native village has since had a nice larger runway built outside of town to replace the old one which ran right through the middle of town. The sizeable dent in the leading edge of the wing was written up as a bird strike to protect the guilty. The fact that the bird was in a tree at the time was not mentioned.

Danger didn't always have to do with being airborne on takeoff and landings. For the loadmaster it was waiting at any of the loading and offloading ventures.

The shift was close to an end, but the air crew decided we could get one more trip in. They didn't ask a worn-out loadmaster what he thought.

The load was two large tanks resembling railroad tanker cars. They were mounted on skids with heavy chains welded between them, so they could be pulled around together. Even empty they were heavy and what was worse was that they were too tall to go in on the rollers and had to be winched in dry, meaning flat on the protective plywood floor.

The tractor trailer with the tanks on backed up to the Herc and we began to winch them on. They would barely move so I poured oil on the plywood where the skids would travel, an old loadmaster trick. It didn't help much because the bottom of the skids was scratched, dented, and otherwise tore up from being skidded around on rocks and gravel.

A front-end loader with forks was needed to push on the tanks while being winched in. This took a lot of time but eventually we had them in. They were chained down, the door shut and well over our duty day time, we headed for Galbraith Lake.

Galbraith Lake was one of the main construction camps during the building of the Alaska pipeline. It was also the site of a major Herc disaster years earlier when a load of gasoline being pumped off caught fire. One man died, three with burns, the loadmaster sustained very severe burns and the Herc was a total loss. It wasn't my favorite place either after this trip.

The ground crew was very proficient and the truck and trailer with the winch cable out and ready were behind the airplane in a couple of minutes. I had the tanks unchained and put the tow chain hook up on the end of the tank to hook the wince cable to. The 25,000 pounds tensile strength Herc chains only have a hook on one end so I hooked a hook to one side of the tank, added a second chain to form a good "V" and a large chain binder to the other end. The chain binder was rated at 26,000-pound strength and had worked well for pulling the tanks in.

The truck driver engaged the winch at my signal as I stood on the ramp making sure the tall tanks slid back as the winch pulled on them barely clearing the door. As the tanks neared the back edge of the ramp the bottom of the skids hung up on the plywood floor creating a much harder pull and the chain binder broke. The chains and winch cable hook hit me in the shins throwing me against the side of the Herc and down to the floor. All this happened before I even heard the sound of the binder breaking.

To say this hurt would be an understatement. I thought both legs and my back were broken, I couldn't move. The ground crew had one man summon the camp ambulance while another went to the cockpit to notify the flight crew. As people gathered around I finally felt like I could move a little. Checking each leg, I discovered that neither felt broke, the ramp floor was slick with ice and snow, and the chains hit so hard they took my feet out from under me. The pain in my back eased a little so I stood up, at least to a monkey position and that was the best I could do.

The flight engineer used to be a loadmaster, so he helped out. The chains were doubled up and the winch cable re-hooked. When the tanks reached the trailer, we could see they were too tall to go on the trailer and would damage the tail section of the Herc. Some days! We decided the tanks would have to go down the ramp onto the ground.

This was easier said than done as the tanks first had to be winched back into the airplane to take the weight off of the tail, so the ramp block could be removed and the ramp lowered to the ground. This was accomplished with the due amount of cussing and the ramp was lowered and truck ramps installed. The huge rig truck and trailer, while spooling out cable, pulled ahead far enough to allow room on the ground for the tanks. Now we were winning, you'd think!

The flight engineer signals the driver to crank in the winch, as the cable tightened the tanks started to move. Though it was pulling hard, it worked fine for a ways. Then the driver stopped the winch, got out of the truck and came back to talk to us. The rough skid bottoms had dug into the plywood floor and the winch truck and trailer were being dragged back toward the airplane instead of the tanks coming out. Now what?!

The rig truck and trailer together weighed a good 75,000 pounds. It was unbelievable they were being dragged across a mixed snow and frozen gravel ramp. A D9 cat was driven up in front of the truck and chained to the truck. Winching was resumed with the tanks finally moving again. This went fine for about a foot then the whole plywood floor inside the Herc started moving. We stopped to check things out and it was decided that the plywood would stop moving when it hit the tie down ring posts screwed into the Herc floor. Sure it would, let's do it. Winching was resumed, when the plywood hit the posts it stopped, and the tanks continued to move, for a few inches that is. Again, the plywood started moving with the tanks shredding the ¾" plywood at all 16 posts it was hitting at the same time.

Enough is enough, and I motioned to the truck driver to keep on winching. He did, and we didn't stop until tanks, plywood, tie down chains, devices, and anything loose was all out on the ground. It looked like a Wile E. Coyote plan on a cartoon, but the tanks were out.

Everything of value was thrown back in on the bare aluminum floor of the Herc and we headed for Fairbanks. I was already on my ambulance. By the time we had taxied to our parking spot at our loading ramp I had become so stiff I could barely move. I lowered the planes ramp to the ground so I could hobble down it. Hoping to hurry up the ground time of a late airplane, the ramp supervisor had pulled up behind the airplane in his pickup to get things moving. The look on his face when he saw the pile of tie down equipment on a bare aluminum floor instead of a ready to go cargo compartment would have made the cover of Life magazine. He was speechless, but I wasn't, as I crawled into the truck I briefly explained what had happened and mentioned it would be a very kindly act to take me to the emergency room for some x-rays.

It turned out nothing was broken, only bruised and a couple days of rest had me back on the job. I was lucky. This was the most serious injury I sustained in many years at this dangerous job.

Danger wasn't always lurking around the airplane, it could crop up anywhere on these worldwide trips. South American taxi-cab rides come to mind first and foremost. After many of these rides I determined that this was the way I would die, long before an airplane crash.

While some of the main streets might have had lane markers and some of the cars turn signals, a ride to the hotel was more like a lineal bumper car ride at the local fair. An elbow out the window was an invitation for a severe bruise. The luxury of riding in the back seat was usually interrupted by a broken shock absorber trying to pass a proctologist exam. Traffic lights of any color either meant to go or go faster. Brakes were a last–minute addition and were only meant to be used at the last possible second. The drivers, I'll admit, were very talented for they had one hand on the shifter, one on the steering wheel, and one on the horn at all times.

Just walking around sightseeing could turn into a life and death situation. One instance was when the mechanic and I were crossing a wide and busy street at a traffic light. We were halfway across when the light changed. Green meant go, and go they did, pedestrians or not. I made it to the curb and turned around just in time to see the mechanic plastered to the front grill of a huge bus and hanging on for dear life. I nervously pranced around waiting for the next light. Sure enough he showed up on my side of the street no worse for the wear.

Santiago, Chile gave the same mechanic and me another sightseeing thrill. Due to scheduling we had a whole day to kill and seeing the sights and investigating local shops was the plan for the day.

While walking the sidewalks two men approached us with an offer to check out their local strip club so we could tell other American tourists about it. We both felt that this fell under the term "sightseeing" and agreed to follow them.

They led us down the street a ways then turned down a side street, halfway down the block one man slid aside a curtain and ushered us in. When my eyes adjusted to the dim light I noticed 4 or 5 men sitting at the bar to our left, the stage was empty and so were all the tables. Being the middle of the day this didn't seem suspicious to us, so we followed the man to the table in front of the stage. He said the girls would be out shortly and asked what we would like to drink. The mechanic ordered a beer and I a coke.

Presently three "girls" showed up and sat down at our table. To say they were "a little worse for the wear" would have been an understatement two decades ago. One look at the mechanic confirmed we would have our drink and leave. The waiter showed up with our drinks, placed them on the table, and said "That will be fifty dollars American."

We both said the drinks and entertainment wasn't worth that and that we were leaving. Halfway to the door the four or five men at the bar suddenly stood up and blocked our way with knives drawn.

Never before, or since, have I wished so much that I was a Kung Fu master and could have kicked the crap out of them. But, alas, I am not. I walked back to the table, laid a fifty-dollar bill down, commented on how pretty the women were and how we'd like to stay, but that we had a pressing engagement and had to leave.

Let's get back to the "safety" of the airplane and leave the dangers of sightseeing to full-fledged tourists.

Once due to the afore mentioned El Nino, we spent a month in Peru. A place that rarely sees rain had had so much that the roads were washed out everywhere. Our job was flying fuel out of Lima to a village high in the Andes Mountains for a nearby gold mine. I was told the mine was owned by the president of Peru and had to stay in operation no matter what. With the roads washed out flying fuel in was the only way to keep the mine operational.

The "no matter what" had us flying in some questionable weather with little navigational aids. On clear days the scenery below was awesome, ranging from ancient Aztec ruins to the beautiful mountains. The village and runway were nestled in a deep green farm studded valley that would be featured in a travel magazine. The runway was a one way in one way out no matter the wind direction due to a mountain that rose up just a few feet from the end of the asphalt.

Except for the occasional turbulence, clear days were delightful flying, the cloudy days were another matter entirely. It was basically flying around looking for a hole in the clouds to get down into the valley and hope the runway wasn't obscured by a lower lying cloud. Many a time we were diving through clouds hopefully to hit the clear air underneath we had glimpsed through a nearby hole. Though sometimes coming out awful close to a mountain we always hit clear air or I wouldn't be writing this now. The thing that made the heart flutter worse was the voice on the reorder of the ground proximity system yelling "Terrain, Terrain" while we were still in a cloud.

Eventually the roads were repaired and off we went looking for flatter ground to fly over.

While flying along many conversations arise as you might imagine. The subjects vary greatly and, in a cockpit, many four letter and "F" words get used. There is however one "F" word that rarely gets used and you never want to hear. That word is "FIRE." One night I had to use it.

We were based out of Detroit flying auto parts to various assembly plants around the country. Some stops were to drop freight off, some to pick-up, some were both and the airplane was always filled to capacity.

On this night we loaded up in Detroit and took some of the cargo to one stop and flew to where I can't remember to pick up more cargo for our destination of Wilmington, Delaware. Most of the cargo was bulky and soon the airplane was near capacity. We put the final oversize pieces on the ramp and secured them. As it was a tight fit I stayed outside on the ground to watch the clearance while the mechanic inside operated the controls to close the ramp and door.

The ramp closed barely with the cargo very close to the ceiling, the door came down and cleared by a quarter inch. Good to go. I walked around the airplane to the crew door and climbed aboard and up the ladder to the cockpit. Knowing the cargo was all secure I didn't do a final walk around check, bad decision.

We cranked up the engines, taxied to the runway, and took off. A half hour into the flight and 29,000 feet in the air my paperwork was finished, the flight crew was doing their various tasks as I reached into my pocket for a cigarette. Damn, the pack was empty, oh well there was more in my flight bag.

My flight bag was in the back against the bulkhead behind the cockpit nice and handy. I got up, went over to the ladder, climbed down and turned left entering the cargo compartment. What met my eyes sent my heart a racing. The back end of the airplane was filled with smoke and I could see the orange glow of fire.

I learned back toward the cockpit and yelled" We got a fire back here!" I grabbed a fire extinguisher and headed down the right side between the cargo and fuselage toward the fire. I looked back to make sure the crew had heard me. The captain was already down the ladder and headed toward me. He was followed closely by the flight engineer and mechanic leaving the co-pilot to fly the airplane.

The flight engineer grabbed another fire extinguisher and with the mechanic following, headed down the left side of the airplane. Though hampered by a narrow passageway, we all made it to the back to find burning pieces of cardboard falling everywhere. The gill liner was burning, and the smoke was so thick we could barely see.

The flight engineer and I started using the extinguishers hitting the gill liner first and then turning to the cardboard. The ramp door was always used for storage of rags, open and full cans of oil and hydraulic fluid and burning cardboard was falling on them. We climbed over burning cargo to get to the flammable liquids while the captain and mechanic barehanded pulled burning cardboard to the floor trying to stomp out the flames. When we were sure the flammable stuff was out and safe we turned the fire extinguishers back on the cardboard to help the captain and mechanic out.

When everything burning was out and safe we collapsed against the fuselage to catch our breath and slow our hearts down to a machine gun rate. It was then that we noticed the smoke detector located on the ceiling right above the fire, it had actually been burning six inches from the detector that had failed to illuminate the light in the cockpit to warn us.

Double checking everywhere around us to make sure nothing was smoldering, we headed back up to the cockpit and a co-pilot scared out of his wits not knowing what was happening in the back. He said he had kept looking over his shoulder at the cock pit entrance to see if flames were licking at his ass.

Ten minutes later I'm not sure we would have gotten the fire out with the extinguishers we had.

All of our Hercs were equipped with extra flood lights mounted to the ceiling over the ramp to facilitate loading operations in the 24 hours of darkness in the Arctic. When the overfull ramp was shut the cardboard boxes ended up to close or even touching these lights which were left on and finally getting so hot they ignited.

Now they say smoking is bad for your health, but I hate to think of what would have happened that night if I hadn't needed a cigarette when I did. With a faulty detector not warning us, once those fluids and aluminum started to burn it could have turned into a real ugly story.

The mechanic was a great guy and a very conscientious worker, but he didn't know what to look for, I did! Though the captain is in charge of the airplane, the cargo compartment was my responsibility. All said and done, in plain English I "F" worded up!

When we landed in Wilmington I went out the crew door and walked to the rear of the airplane where behind a little door are controls to operate the ramp and door from the outside. You should have seen the looks on the faces of the ground crew as the ramp lowered. Charred cardboard and melted tail light lenses were falling to the ground on both sides of the ramp. This was not our standard operating procedure for delivering cargo.

In recent years here in Alaska the Herc hasn't been called on to haul fuel very often. The reliable old DC-6s and DC-4s can haul fuel a lot cheaper and mostly keep up with the demand in Alaska's remote places.

During the oil pipeline construction and oil exploration days it was a different story. Fuel hauls were a major portion of our requested loads. We could change over from hauling "dry" to fuel tanker in about an hour's time. The 4 fuel tanks were mounted on a framework with wheels that raised and lowered and were easily winched into the aircraft. The tie down took up most of the time.

It was a hot, muggy time in July. The temperature was in the 90's, about as hot as it ever gets in Fairbanks. This kind of weather had an adverse effect on the performance of an airplane. You could really notice this in the Herc as opposed to a -40° clear day in the winter.

"You have N106 today, it's tanked up for fuel" the ramp supervisor informed as I stirred my morning coffee.

"O.K, I can handle that" was my reply.

N106AK was my favorite airplane and the one I had the most time on. Consequently, the one I had the most mishaps on, say like a fire. I learned some years ago it now lies at the bottom of a ravine in Africa, beyond repair after running off a runway.

Hauling diesel fuel was smelly, but it was a lot easier work than most dry loads and was considered by most loadmasters as an easy day. Life was good, favorite airplane, easy loads, all right.

I grabbed my flight bag and walked across the ramp to where the airplane was parked. Damn, it was hot already. The fuel truck pulled up to the rear of the plane just as I got there. We hooked up the hoses and began pumping on the 7,200 gallons that was our usual load.

Fuel trips were priced by the gallons, the more gallons, the more money. For that reason, it also made them one of our heaviest loads. Making money was the name of the game, even if it took a little pencil whipping to keep the FAA ignorant and happy.

The flight crew showed up just as I unhooked the hose and shut the ramp and door. I climbed the walkway between the tops of the tanks and made my way to the cockpit. We went through the usual amenities. "This is what we get for a loadmaster?" Answered by, "you know how to drive this thing?"

We taxied to the runway, turned on it, put on full power and roared toward take off. Using a lot of runway, we finally lifted off. Hundreds of feet in the air and just past the end of the runway we lost an engine. It was shut down and the prop quickly feathered as we ceased to gain altitude and were barely staying airborne.

Normal procedure was to cross the Tanana River and dump wing fuel before returning to land. That wasn't happening! Pigs wallow in the mud for pleasure and you enjoy wallowing around in a hot tub but wallowing around in the air hundreds of feet above the ground is anything but fun!

You could feel it in the seat of your pants as the airplane dipped and shuddered. I can only imagine what the yoke must have felt like in the pilot's hands. With ¼ of our power gone at the worst possible time we were clawing air to stay flying. Every second felt like that was the last we would stay in the air.

Turning to get back to the runway took away some of our lift but had to be done. We circled around to the runway, that black, beautiful, white stripped, solid runway. No time for waiting red lights this time. The pilot was soaking wet with sweat as we all were to some extent, but I believe you could have actually wrung water out of his.

We couldn't thank Jim Davies enough as he parked the Herc in front of the hangar for an engine change. We went our separate ways, me to finish out the day building loads and then to the nearest bar.

The mechanics took over and proceeded to change out the engine. By the next morning the new engine was on and had been run up, so the airplane was ready to go again.

"You got 106 again, do it right this time," were the words I heard from the ramp supervisor that next morning. "No problem" was my reply. As the fuel load was still on board we were soon ready to leave. Engines were cranked up and we headed to the runway.

We roared down the runway on another hot July day lifting off at the halfway point. Just clearing the end of the runway, we lost a different engine.

Not again! The same decision was made to nix dropping fuel, we needed back on the runway and soon! We wallowed around and lined up on the runway. I believe it looked even prettier today. I couldn't begin to tell you how good it felt to be standing on solid ground instead of in a seat that could fall out from under you at any second.

The mechanics came through and next morning, N106AK was ready to go. "Do it until you get it right" were the encouraging words I heard that morning. Off I went with the best of intentions, after all two days in a row, what were the odds?

It wasn't long until we were roaring down the runway, props biting all the hot air they could grab. Moments after liftoff, one of the two old engines quit.

You know the drill by now, you also know we made it again or you wouldn't be reading this.

The next morning before the ramp supervisor said anything I said, "I'll be working the ground today, thank you." I didn't get any argument.

By this time the mechanics knew something was terribly wrong. After much searching, the culprit was found. N106AK had somehow been filled with contaminated fuel. Why two engines didn't quit at the same time is beyond me. The tanks and fuel lines were drained and flushed out and the airplane was refueled. That morning N106AK took off just fine and flew fuel loads all day. The only thing missing was one horribly hungover loadmaster.

My memory fails me as to who the other flight crew was, all I remember is it was the same crew for two days and another on the third day. You find somebody else in aviation who has had three engine failures in a row.

It was El Nino weather that brought us to Papua, New Guinea in '97. Normally one of the wettest places in the world, it was bone dry. Forest fires were everywhere, and the smoke was so thick it was affecting a large portion of the globe.

The mine was located in the mountains in the interior of P.N.G. and was normally supplied by barges pushed up the river to the mines base camp. This river was now just a trickle and the smoke lay heavy over it and the nearby mountains.

Tabubil was owned and run by an Australian mining firm and employed and took care of 40,000 natives in the immediate area. With only a trail for a road to the village of Kianga they were desperate for food and other supplies. In total we airlifted 7.5 million pounds of supplies to the mine.

The runway was gravel and of sufficient size but was located on a bench along the river in a narrow valley surrounded by tall mountains. The only way in was to follow the river until you could see a vast area of shipping containers and then find the runway uphill beyond. We were told the mountain sides were littered with airplanes that didn't make it to the runway. Too much information dude!

There was no go around for this airstrip. Well there was, for small airplanes and Australian Hercs which we were told only hauled 4,000 pounds at a time so they could go around. We weren't allowed that luxury. With the shipping containers weighing between forty and forty-seven thousand pounds, a few miles down the valley we were committed to land, or crash, take your pick.

The mines project manager greeted us each morning with "Four for sure." On a good day we could fly four trips, on a bad day only one, depending on how thick the forest fire smoke was. Each trip was a loaded container in and an empty one for backhaul. With temperatures always around 100° F this made for a hard day's work.

Here in the U.S. I.F.R. means "instrument flight rules" that is used in bad weather. Over there it meant "I follow river," it was the only navigational aid we had.

Some days we couldn't even find the river out on flatter terrain to turn and follow it into the mountains. On better days we'd spot the dry gravel river bed and lower down and try and keep it in sight as we meandered through the mountains. The smoke was like flying through clouds, thicker in places than other, but ever present. Many was the times for short periods we'd look out the windshield and see nothing, sometimes not even the river bed below. Then come into a patch of lighter smoke to get our bearings. What set the pulse to racing were the times we would see nothing ahead, but off to the sides not far past the wing tips, the lush green foliage covering the mountainsides.

On the North Slope we had the times of white-outs for a while, but here the relentless smoke was day after day. I don't know how the other guys felt, but to me the feeling was something akin to what World War II bomber crews must have felt like before each mission. Were we coming home after this trip? What we did wasn't near as dangerous, but it wasn't your drive to the beach either.

We loaded up and fueled up that day the same as any other, taxied out and took off. It was about a 45-minute flight from the coastal town of Wewak where we were based to the mine of Tabubil. The smoke was thicker than usual when we found the riverbed and headed up the valley. When we knew the runway was getting close the co-pilot hit the lever to drop the landing gear. It went down, but the right main gear indication light didn't come on. The gear was quickly recycled and this time the light came on, then flickered and went out, came back on and out again.

The light kept flickering, but at that point it didn't matter, we were well past the pull up point and we were landing or crashing. The captain made a good landing and as we rolled out not applying the brakes any more than needed the gear held.

After a few loud sighs and the defibrillator used on me we off loaded the airplane on the runway not wanting to take the chance of collapsing the gear taxing to the ramp. Everything came off fine and of course nothing went back on.

Now came the only time in my career that we chained the landing gear down. This was something that was usually done in the air before landing. I've talked to very few people who have ever had to do this, it was a rarity and the Herc was one of a few airplanes that had the option for this to be done.

We removed the panels from inside the cargo compartment by the wheel wells to access the gear struts. We hooked the chains around the struts and ran them to the tie down rings inside in a "X" pattern. Secondary chains were applied over the first chains and we were ready to go.

We flew back to Wewak with the gear down and had the mechanics take over. The reason the gear was hung up was a rag wound up in the jackscrew. One of the hired local natives had left a rag lying in the wheel well after cleaning up. During takeoff the rag must have blew onto the jackscrew, stuck to the grease and wound up in the cylinder when the landing gear was retracted. A little detail missed leading to a big and potentially disastrous event. Let's go back to Alaska for one last story.

Problems seem to arise on airplanes all of a sudden, no warning, no time or way to correct, often leading to disaster. This instance was one of those and though it barely felt like anything because conditions stayed right, it could have been disastrous.

Point Hopes lies on a narrow gravel spit jutting out into the Beaufort Sea on the north-west coast of Alaska. Cold and windy most of the time, it seems like a most inhospitable place to live, but many Eskimos called it home.

This was a normal trip hauling a skid load of building materials in normal conditions. We descended and made our approach to the runway; the wind was blowing like hell and lots of left rudder was needed to keep us in line with the runway. All of a sudden, the rudder stuck in the full left position as we neared the runway. If the wind would have died just then we couldn't have landed or stayed flying.

Luckily the wind stayed steady until we touched down, there wasn't any gust or lulls, like the wind always does there. Once on the ground the pilot kept us straight with engine power adjustments until we slowed down enough so the nose wheel steering could be used. Like I said it didn't feel like much, but it could just as easily have been disastrous.

The mechanic on board diagnosed the problem, got on the phone, and ordered the parts needed for repair. They wouldn't arrive until the next afternoon, so we had some time to fill. We managed to find accommodations in a closed down hotel and even a hot meal that night.

Point Hope is thought by many to be the oldest permanent habitation location in North America. The next morning, we wandered about taking in the town and then hiking out the road to the runway and the spit. Along the way was the graveyard surrounded with a fence made entirely out of whale rib bones standing on end. Inside we followed the headstones back to the late 1700's before the inscriptions became too worn and weathered to read. Still the headstones went on.

Past the forlorn Herc setting on the end of the gravel runway were the centuries old sod huts used by the Eskimos for generations. Slowly more modern buildings were put up farther back on the mainland until oil money allowed a massive building project in the 1980's.

Off to our left was some kind of celebration going on so we strolled over to see what was going on. The wind was blowing, and it was cold, but it had little effect on the hardy Eskimos. Some had little driftwood fires going behind the shelter of a rock pile, others had seal skins propped up as windbreakers looking like umbrellas on a California beach.

On the leeward side of a seal skin was something I hadn't seen since my childhood days. There was on elderly man with his family gathered around. In the middle propped up and leveled on some rocks was a carom board. When they saw me, the man motioned me to kneel down and challenge him to a game.

I accepted and knelt down. It had to have been over 30 years since I had played this game, but I still expected to make a decent showing. Screw "Minnesota" have you ever heard of "Eskimo Fats." If I had been betting he would have soon been the proud owner of a Herc and we would have been walking home.

That afternoon the airplane with our parts showed up and we were back in operation. On the flight back to Fairbanks I found myself reflecting on the adventures and opportunities this job had presented me over the years.

Drill Rig in the Middle of Nowhere

CHAPTER 7 - FINAL APPROACH

never did like the term "final approach," who came up with that anyway? Whoever it was wasn't with us on our fifth go around looking for an ice strip in a whiteout or rolling out applying max power to take off again because we had landed too far down the runway to stop. It makes it sound like this is it and we are down for good. Maybe it's from the old-time pilots who considered it a good landing if you walked away from it and an excellent landing if you were able to use the airplane again.

I recall one landing that might be considered a final approach.

It was cold, extremely that winter day in Fairbanks. The thermometer read -50° F as I pulled into work that evening. That kind of weather will shut down a lot of airplanes, but not a Herc, I've been flying at -70° F or colder.

We loaded up and headed north to an unremembered destination, dropped the load off, and headed back to Fairbanks. It had turned colder while we were gone, it was -55°F and the ice fog had thickened. When we came over the hills north of town you could see the whole Tanana Valley was socked in and Fairbanks Int'l wouldn't let us try an approach.

This presented a problem as Anchorage, 300 miles away was listed on our flight plan as our alternate before leaving Fairbanks. Because of a couple go arounds to land at our North Slope destination and unforeseen head winds we didn't have enough fuel to make it to Anchorage.

We were instructed to head to Eielson Air force base 30 miles southeast of Fairbanks because of their fantastic radar capabilities. The radar did prove to be fantastic. When they told us we were lined up on the runway a couple of miles out we let down the landing gear and set the flaps to 100% and descended through the fog. They talked us in all the way down and beyond. The air traffic controller said, "You're on line fifty feet above the runway, forty, thirty, ten; you should touch down about now." Bump! We were there! As we slowed down controller said, "Your veering left, turn right a little, that's good, hold steady, we'll send out a "follow me truck."

Sitting higher in the air than the truck we could still not see the runway or taxi lights. The only thing visible was the flashing yellow beacon on the truck that led us at last to a parking spot. What a feeling, landing blind and surviving! Let's don't do it again!

Looking back, this job, the Hercs, the travel, all began because of oil. If oil hadn't been discovered in the remote Arctic regions of Alaska none of this would have happened to me and many others. I started out in this book to mostly narrate the story of the Herc and its job pertaining to the development of the Trans Alaska Pipeline, but the book ended up, like me, going places I never thought I would go.

I doubt there isn't one of the first workers on the Slope who doesn't have a Herc story. They have told me how they loved seeing a Herc roar in through the blowing snow bringing in everything they needed to keep working and living. Always were they amazed at how much and what objects it could haul. I believe the Herc's airlift capabilities took a year or twos time off from the actual pumping of oil as opposed to waiting for the Haul road to be built before they could start.

If someone would have told me as a kid growing up on a dairy farm that I would see as much of the world as I have, I would have wondered what he was putting in his milk. A lot of kids have a career in mind at a young age. I wasn't one of them. I only knew I wouldn't be milking cows at 5 AM. I even came to Alaska with the idea of working the summer and going back to school. That didn't work out and I never went back to school, you can probably tell. Offhand I couldn't come up with a job that suited me better than being a loadmaster.

I'll admit there were times I wondered what the hell I was doing, but there were also the times I wondered how I could be so lucky as to be where I was. It wasn't what you would call a prestigious job, but you could feel proud of what you had accomplished. Some people treated us loadmasters like a dumb animal; actually, for the most part we were fairly smart animals. The job took a lot of improvising and foresight at times. Some people had the resourcefulness, and some didn't and couldn't cut it. Some people were scared to death and quit, others just got gray hair and changed underwear a lot.

Aviation as a whole is an industry with tremendous ups and downs. One month the future looks bright, the next, you're in the unemployment line. At times we could use more Hercs to do all the work available, at times there wasn't enough room to park them. Boom or bust, an Alaskan tradition since it was discovered.

As far as the Hercs future, I can't see the world without them. They are almost always the first airplane called in when there is a disaster or situation. Whether a military or civilian occurrence the C-130 Hercules will always be needed and will perform with the ability and reliability few aircraft could achieve. When the news media tells you that a cargo or search aircraft is on the way, you can bet it's a Herc to the rescue. It's the first thing the Coast Guard sends out for a search and rescue. It will be the first airplane in with needed supplies to an earthquake shortened runway. It will be the transportation called on for a paratrooper jump or supplies to be air dropped. Remember, it was a Herc to the rescue in the movie Air Force One.

For as long as Hercs continue to operate there will be a need for talented and courageous pilots and crewmembers. Loadmasters worth their salt are a must. So, if you are half monkey, enjoy long hours, getting hurt, having the crap scared out of you, and rarely seeing home, be sure to get your application in.

This was an occupation that was rough on families. The many days spent away from home, the unpredictable departures and long hours were the cause of many divorces. I've heard of people just sitting down to Christmas dinner when the phone rang, and the husband and father is called away on a hot trip. Occurrences like this, spoiling plans, add up and are certainly not conducive to a good family life. Myself, I missed out on a lot of seeing my kids grow up. All their "firsts" were during the big push for oil on the North Slope and I was constantly gone.

The job of loadmaster required always learning new things by the very nature of the job. Two of the most important things I learned flying on the Slope were: (1) You do not squeeze on a Capri-Sun pouch while inserting the straw and (2) you never, but never, no matter how big of a hurry you're in, put your belt with a heavy brass buckle through two belt loops and yank it through, where the buckle can hit you puts a stop to all proceedings, I from experience, can guarantee it.

It took a long time to learn what clothes to pack. In northern Alaska on any given winter day the record high and low temperature can vary as much as 100°F. Between that and suddenly changed destinations it's a crap shoot. I have had a bag of clothes packed for working in the Canadian arctic and ended up being sent to Africa. On that occasion the company was nice enough to give me some money to purchase the appropriate clothes. The worst was the time I ended up in Hawaii dressed in a flannel shirt, long johns top and bottom, and insulated boots with only the clothes on my back. I sure received some funny looks in the hotel's gift store when I purchased sandals, shorts, and a T-shirt and changed out right there. They did stop me when I started on the shorts, no sense of humor.

I'm too old now to be doing the job of loadmaster, I'm not tough enough to be throwing around 180-pound rollers nor could I handle the long and often very cold hours it requires. But I did have a few years left in me when, due to circumstances beyond my control, I lost my career in aviation. It seems some Canadian, (we won't mention any country names), upon checking, found out I had a couple of DUI's many years prior when I was a wild and crazy kid and would no longer be allowed in their country.

I went on for a good while sneaking in and out before they realized I had been there. This did not endear me any to the customs agent. Finally, the computer age caught up to me and they knew I was coming in before I landed there. The R.C. M.P. and customs agent reception when I stepped out of the crew door did justice to a full-fledged terrorist. I was informed if I ever showed up again I would go to jail. Not my favorite chain of hotels.

I knew when I told my boss about this that I'd probably lose my job. The company applied for a permit that cost me $200.00, but even the letter from the president of the company saying I was a valued employee and not a crazy kid anymore and would appreciate their consideration in the matter didn't help.

Since this would cause a major problem on an aircraft flying around looking for work I was considered a liability and was terminated. Seems to me there was a lot of the world, left to fly to, but that was the decision.

I'm still not allowed in Canada which puts me on a very long list of Americans in the same boat. This means I can't drive the Alcan Highway and have to fly to the Lower 48. I've heard that some "outlaws" are able to drive the highway by buying a two to four-hundred-dollar permit. They are suddenly an acceptable person. We've been all over Africa and South American and have learned that "greasing the palm" works wonders when nothing else will. All third world countries operate that way.

When I lost my job, I lost a good paying and an interesting one that fit me to a "T." I was very grateful to have had the chance to do the things we've done and see the places we have been, I'll miss that always. The hard work they can keep.

It works both ways though; the Herc and its work duties lost a good man. Many of the flight crew members and people I've worked with would, if asked, tell you that. You might even hear that from my former boss, of course you would have to catch him on a good day, in a good mood, after a good meal, good luck! Most likely though he would be remembering things like that trip to Columbia.

It wasn't a special trip by any means, just a normal everyday affair. We loaded up in Houston, Texas, a G.E. generator if I remember right and headed south for Bogota, Columbia. Everything went well the whole trip, nothing unusual.

We offloaded the generator onto a trailer, fueled up, and headed back to the U.S. It was while I was gathering all the paperwork up that I realized I had forgotten to have the airway bill signed. No problem, I just wrote down a Spanish sounding name and gave all the paperwork to the co-pilot who was responsible for getting it back to the company. Done deal.

It was a few days later sitting in a company apartment in Ypsilanti, MI where we were based at the time when the phone rang. It was the boss back in Anchorage and started out with the usual amenities.

"Hello."

"*#$%^#^ it Tupper"

"Oh, hi Jerry, what's up?

"Damn it! How many times have I told you to make sure the airway bill gets signed?"

"About three hundred seventy-four I think. Why, did I miss one?"

"That Columbia trip last week."

"It was signed."

"Do you expect me to believe that Juan Valdez signed that airway bill?"

"I was hoping..."

"Damn it, that's what we get paid from is the airway bill, you make sure they get signed from now on!

"So, three hundred seventy-five then...?"

CLICK!!!

O.K. Jerry you got me on that one, Juan Valdez didn't sign that airway bill, his donkey did. He was a right smart donkey.

THE END

We hope you enjoyed this book.

The author and publisher would greatly appreciate an honest review.

Thank you!

ABOUT THE AUTHOR

Born and raised on a dairy farm in northern Minnesota, the author came to Alaska in 1969. The first seven years were spent as a meat cutter which became rather boring. He fell into aviation in 1977 and was on or around airplanes for the next 40 years. He felt it was the best job he could have had and had a lot of experiences he hopes you find enjoyable reading.

Other Titles available from
ALASKA DREAMS PUBLISHING
www.alaskadp.com

Legend Of Silene

Apache Snow

In Search of Honor

A Coming Storm

Arizona Rangers Series – Blake's War

My Life In The Wilderness

All Over The Road

Ghost Cave Mountain

Inside the Circle

The Silver Horn of Robin Hood

Alaskan Troll Eggs

Through My Eyes

The Professional Ghost Investigator

The Adventures of Jason and Bo

Please visit www.alaskadp.com and sign up for the ADP mailing list to be notified of future titles by Alaska Dreams Publishing.

Made in the
USA
Monee, IL